Forgiving Tabitha

Marcy Lanes

Rev. date: 06/03/2021

To order additional copies of this book, contact:
Xlibris
844-714-8691
www.Xlibris.com
Orders@Xlibris.com
821670

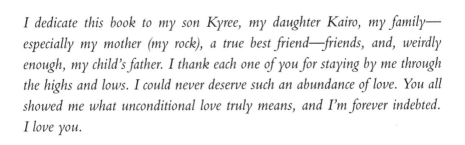

I dedicate this book to my son Kyree, my daughter Kairo, my family—especially my mother (my rock), a true best friend—friends, and, weirdly enough, my child's father. I thank each one of you for staying by me through the highs and lows. I could never deserve such an abundance of love. You all showed me what unconditional love truly means, and I'm forever indebted. I love you.

Introduction

Maybe you're wondering if you're about to read another book about pity, forgiveness, and all is well, then please put this book down. I have ended here by no coincidence at all. Neither have you. You're either here by support, curiosity, or you want to redeem yourself by forgiveness. I want to tell you a story about a woman who's from southwest Washington, DC. On the surface, she is family oriented, hardworking, and college educated. Deep down inside is her alter ego, who's money driven, self-centered, and emotionally scared. She left behind trails of new beginnings and failed relationships—whether it was family, men, or friends. She remained unbothered due to her unwanted genes of a sociopath. Is forgiveness on the table?

A part of my life I claimed to be dead has risen. I have buried, disposed, and somehow forgotten it for quite a while. Yet, I've mourned for the last fourteen years. How do you mourn for something or someone who's alive? You drink and make up the rules as you go. The world owed me! Hell, everybody owed me. At least that's how I saw it. I had too many losses not to get what I deserved or be entitled. What the world would call a profound, happy, little girl is now . . . well, I'll let you read it.

For a whole year and a couple of months, I manually wrote about everything that happened to me, from fainting to recovery. Now, thinking you have no idea how I ended here, huh? I'll give you the adult chapter of my life for now. I was eighteen years old when I got pregnant. I was scared shitless. Barely knew the difference between circumcised and uncircumcised, and here I was on the verge of being someone's mother. First time in eighteen years I fell in love with someone other than me. I wasn't even sure I wanted to tell the father. I'm a firm believer that both parties should have a right in deciding the best choice for the baby. But I was already in love with Kairo. This guy and I weren't exactly in a relationship, but love was ultimately a thing. We were always together; our smiles always spoke so many words, and I would just smile and giggle at the mention of his name. We made moves together during "drug missions." I never got a chance to tell him. He just disappeared with no trace of him. That following Sunday, I remember going to church with my family. I passed a note asking if they told anyone about the baby because I wasn't ready to tell anyone yet. Let's just say, by the end of the day, everyone knew about the baby. We all have that one family member that can't hold water or like to see you in pieces, because the attention is off them or some people enjoy other people's misery. They were waiting for me to say something. Their minds were preset for judgment due to my prior decisions of how I was living. I would be laughing and joking, making to-do plans for tomorrow, knowing I would be gone for the next few days. But that's how I got by—living in the moment and manipulating the situation. No one was surprised because it was already known I was the black sheep.

All at the same time this other guy that I was dating at the time was cheating on me with some chick that attended the same school and lived in a nearby neighborhood. I loved school, but I choose my family affairs over it. Here, I was in my senior year taking senior pictures, knowing I probably wouldn't finish because I had my uncle on my mind. I finished. Money was always a priority for me; I hated struggling or penny-pinching. I was offered room and board for free, clean clothes, food, and some small change in my pocket. I chose my family because I was taught family always come first. While I was looking out for family, the pieces of me were slowly chipping away. I always looked at things through my own window. I felt disconnected anyway, so I took the opportunity to distance myself further to come up with a master plan on how I was going to change the world. No. I wasn't planning on building a drug empire. I had other dreams. What a way to start, right? The guy I was dating at the time was my first real boyfriend. We dated for three years. The first two years we made out, kissing and hugging. It was the week before I turned eighteen that I let my best friend take my virginity. I remember the day we met: His big brown eyes were charming, and he had a sense of humor to match. We were crazy about each other until we were no longer enough for us. After some time passed, we both wanted more. We were barely talking, yet spending time together. Don't get me wrong, we truly loved each other at one point, but we were kids. We were drifting apart, and neither of us wanted to be the first to say it was over. Everyone knew us. We were always together. Most people would call this their most embarrassing moment ever, but for me, it was a huge relief when everything came out around our city that he had another girl pregnant. Everyone was talking, whispering, and staring, but I remained calm because I knew I was out of the woods. Crazy part the guy I was actually pregnant by got locked up. I didn't even know until a year and a half later. I thought he just up and disappeared and didn't care about what we had. But anyhow, later that night, my boyfriend at the time called and promised to take care of the baby, even if I were to decide that I didn't want to be together anymore. I was happy he made the choice for me by cheating and getting caught, but at the same time in disbelief about how I no longer had to tell him because his shit spilled out first. I lost the baby though. I had to have a DNC. I felt it when I lost my baby. I saw it with my own eyes. Pure gold with wings, leaving my body. It literally felt like someone was snatching a soul out of me.

I had a dream I had a painful miscarriage. I went to the bathroom and there was blood. No pain, but it felt like a nightmare. I went to the emergency room. They searched for the baby's heartbeat, but nothing. I had a ruthless foreign doctor tell me straight up, "The baby is dead. You need to have a DNC tomorrow morning or Monday." I was completely withdrawn. I choose Monday because I wanted to believe that a miracle would happen over the weekend, and they were wrong about not hearing my baby's heartbeat. After hours of unsettled tears and confusion, my mom finally convinced me to do it sooner than later. I never loved someone so much I never met. I felt so guilty over my baby's death. Granted, I did nothing wrong, but explain to the woman carrying a little human being inside of her that the baby is no longer living. Do you really think we blame nature? I was scrambling eggs and cooking grits when it happened. My mom came to visit. I was six months pregnant, and she never touched my stomach. I think she knew. We all have these weird visions in my immediate family, not like we're psychic, but we just know something before it happens. It's a feeling of knowing. We can't tell you who, but the scenario is correct. I was scrambling eggs when suddenly a strong urge of pressure was pulling from my body. My mom asked, "What's wrong?" I told her, but she never looked shocked or surprised. I never skip a word when I tell about what happened that day. It still hurts though it's easier to live through now. I never got the chance to talk about it. People immediately started telling me how lucky I was and how I had the chance to start over again, that I wouldn't be trapped with a baby. I was still high off the drugs from the hospital. How do you start over after death? I never did tell my boyfriend at the time the truth. He was there and waited after the surgery with my mom. I felt that was the least he could do after the surface humiliation for me; we broke up and moved on. I couldn't handle the stupidity stares and embarrassment. Well, at least he did. That fool got a bunch of kids. I was left with shattered pieces and secrets.

I aimlessly walked around like everything was okay. I was crushed, but I let other people's opinions dictate how I should've felt. On the outside, I was hanging on, but the inside was slowly dying and I entered the darkest place of my life, yet I was existing. A year or so passed and I was pregnant again. OMG! The conversations about me were sickening from people who I thought would never do that. I was not ready, but I was grateful to be pregnant because my doctor said it would be difficult, but God always has the last word. The announcement of my second pregnancy was also done in the same matter, except this time it was immediately directed to the whole neighborhood without warning or permission to broadcast my private life. During my pregnancy, everything was wonderful. It was after my baby was born that things changed. I had no idea about postpartum depression. Birth comes with no manual. Toxic became my new norm. It was my relationships. It was my only relationship. I used to smoke weed daily. After my son was born, I wanted to smoke because I haven't done it in so long. I wanted something from my past to make sense. Epic fail! I was so high, I never wanted to do that again. I said maybe I should just have a drink. I was *never* a drinker. I would choose smoking over drinking any day. But that day I decided to drink. Boy, did I enjoy the way it made me feel. It numbed all the pain and silenced the secrets that spoke louder than any other words. I wanted more, and hard liquor was now my new best friend. I stopped talking and started drinking. I would be so drunk, I couldn't even remember how I got home most days. I just remember waking up late and my son was hungry. I had major hangovers. A complete loser/friend at the time told me how to get rid of a hangover. Oh! Wow, now I could drink as much as I wanted because I knew how to fix a hangover. Let's just say I was historically drunk for the next eleven years. I even spent the night in jail due to alcohol and poor decisions. The sight of runny eggs and raw sausages should have woken any person up. I looked around at the other women and had the audacity to judge them, thinking to myself this was a mistake. I don't belong here, I'm too good for this, and these women are pathetic. Crackheads, thieves, prostitutes, and users. It didn't stop me though.

There was this one guy named Marcell. He was exceptionally smart in school. I never paid him much attention in school if we were talking about looks. I thought he was cute, but I admired his ability to grasp things so quickly, especially in math class. As we became adults, I saw him again and he told a mutual friend he always had a crush on me. I finally decided to take him up on his offer of dating. We never really did date, but we had one thing in common: *money*. I would ride with him as he would get boosters to steal from different stores. We would wait a few days, sometimes weeks, before we would return the items for cash. Usually, we would take our cut right after the transaction was done, but I wanted to seem green, so he would give me what he wanted to, and I would just accept it. I knew that look in his eyes, he thought he found a sucker. I wasn't interested in his chump change. I read his style years ago. He kept money at home.

I was invited back to his place, which wasn't his—it clearly was a functioning crackhead house. He supplied the drugs, and they gave him a home. We partied all night. I made it my mission to slowly sip on this weak wine all night and feel a buzz as I eyed his money drawer. After putting him to sleep and confirming his snore, I made my withdrawals. I did this for months on end. He would always complain how he had to grind harder because his money wasn't stacking fast enough. I made $7,500 of being green to the eye. Eventually, I got bored with the slow scams. I accidentally fell in love with a wonderful guy. He loved my mom and his, but he was obsessed with making her proud. He could never do enough because she always wanted more. His dad wasn't around, so it was like he was her husband. He was a woman saver. Well, at least that's how it came off. He was always helping women with their problems regardless of the time of night. It made me uncomfortable. I guess I could have said something, but I sabotaged the relationship anyway. My drinking was a problem I couldn't hide from, no matter how far I traveled. He was husband material though. He opened doors, pulled out chairs, took me on romantic dates, helped with my son. Money was so easy, I never had to ask—it was giving with pleasure. I've always worked so my money was mine. I tried to stop drinking with two weeks of success. I thought I could casually drink. What a joke I played on myself. I made so many promises to my family that I'll stop drinking. I honestly wanted to; I just couldn't stop at the time. I never knew alcoholism was a sickness until it happened to me. I went to so many Alcoholic Anonymous meetings. I wanted to believe I was the person who got up and shared her story and everyone would be proud of me, but I sat in my chair, making mental notes and thinking of new ways to bullshit and manipulate my family so I could drink in peace. I was a half-ass functioning alcoholic. I knew not to come to work drunk. I wanted the money to support my habit. I hated asking people for anything. I couldn't tell you if it was my pride or the fact that I needed my habit done right my way with my own money. I remember my aunt telling me, when I first started smoking cigarettes, you better make sure you can support your own habits. Ever since then, I always made sure I had enough for my alcohol and cigarettes. It was the new package deal with me. My son, cigarettes, alcohol, and me. If guys wanted to talk to me, they had to have money and get cigarettes and alcohol to be in my presence along with other mandatory necessities. It was nothing special about the guys I used to talk to. It was for my toxic purposes only. I must say through it all, I must have had a wonderful spirit under the damaged goods because I came across some great guys, some whom I'm still friends with today. A lot of my so-called friendships with women were built off alcohol. They enjoyed the perks of the game I ran on men, except they got caught up with the glitz and glam. I don't hang with any of them no more. They either got more kids than they wanted or stuck in abusive relationships. I see a few of them in the streets every now and then. Only words exchange is "Hey, gurl." Normally, you wouldn't speak to people who helped you down a destructive path. But you must respect the street codes. These women still hold my secrets, as I do theirs. I must say I'm rather shocked it's some things I never heard and much I never told. I missed opportunities because I was drunk, not like I showed up drunk. I was too drunk to do anything, or I blacked out and I couldn't get up. The excuses I used to use to get out of things were ridiculous and doleful, but it worked. I had never been written up or fired from any job. I was mostly a weekend alcoholic. I worked hard all week and anticipated when Friday came, I would binge-drink until Sunday afternoon. It would take me two to three days to fully recover. But I started changing my patterns so it would look like I'm not doing the same thing every weekend. Sometimes, I still believe my old co-workers knew I was drinking. Hell, it's not that hard to realize when someone has a hangover at work. They didn't care about it if it didn't interfere with their hours or money. They weren't bothered. I've been going back and forth about how honest I wanted to be with you, but the truth is how honest am I willing to be to myself. I was horrible back then. I blamed everyone and more, mainly because I disappointed myself putting other people's needs before mine. My father always told me I was leader. Which I am—I just wanted to see what life was like if

I chose someone other than me. Some people were jackasses though. Don't misunderstand, I've done some things, but that doesn't mean I didn't come across some mean-hearted spirits too. Some people will disturb your peace to see you shattered. This one guy I knew, knew how to make my life a living hell. He made good on his promise too. He had someone close in my family who helped him. They're still connected to this day. Crazy part, neither one knows I know. I'll let the sleeping bear sleep for now. Years of unnecessary torture. We both played a part in self-destruction. We fought. I'm talking about punches landed, knives and gun play, depending on how drunk I was and how high he felt, yelled, talked, loved, and hated. He even slept with a few of those so-called friends. Recalling this one chick, I remember her eyes were always to the side and her handshake was too soft. Everyone real know a handshake is supposed to be firm. Basically, acknowledging you're solid. Her cousin had heart, she knew the game, she was real, but she introduced us mainly because we were closer in age. That tells you everything you need to know: Solid don't come with age. I partially blame myself. I invited them to candyland with free passes. We did this for years. After some years passed, he reached out to me hoping to get a better relationship, but he didn't change. I didn't change much myself. I just preferred not to deal with it anymore. So I walked away from the possibility of not knowing what could have been. He wasn't all bad. We had some amazing times together. I do believe we were two broken people trying to glue together what we didn't have to give. His pain was physical, and mine was emotional. I will always have a certain level of love, but never enough to give myself in that manner again. A lot of our behavior was displayed in front of my son. I thought I was sheltering him from some things, but I was surprised to find out how much he already knew. Please be mindful. Kids know way more than we ever could think. I must be careful when I say guys I dated. Most were guys I used to get what I wanted. I had no intentions of ever being with anyone, except one guy I fell in love with, but I sabotaged it because I knew I couldn't give that kind of love at that time. I've told men all kind of lies. I created dreams that I wanted for myself.

I knew how to sound convincing, but not overboard. I used to talk such a good game. I had men invested in businesses that weren't even existing. My addiction meant the world to me. Everything was okay, or at least that's what it felt like in the moment. I hated myself inside and out. But I used my outside appearance to get me by. I can see you now eyeballing the page to see if I'll admit to sleeping with any of them. I'll let your imagination have fun with that. People told me all the time how pretty I was. I just couldn't grasp it at the time, because I was on my own emotional roller coaster. Inside I was dying, and alcohol changed that with every sip. Once I felt warm, everything was okay and I felt like I could conquer the world. Except the world wasn't enough. I started moving drugs out of state. I never touched it, but I was paid damn good to ride two cars behind to make sure everything went smooth. Or become plan B for a distraction. Some say they never regretted anything that happened in life. I would be a liar if I said the same. I totally regret not giving my son the love, respect, and nourishment he deserved growing up. That's my hardest truth. Saying it out loud, I wasn't the best mother to my son at that time. I overcompensated for the lack of attention, and I would try to smooth over my bullshit with expensive shoes and clothes. I would buy game systems—anything that would bounce attention away from me being an irresponsible parent at the time I did, except I wasn't bouncing attention away. I was creating someone to be just like me. I told/tell him I love him every day, but every day was never enough to get myself together. Now, I'm trying to tie up loose endings. A lot of pain my son suffered I created, along with others' absence. Just like the choices I made. Some things you can't control, but I had a chance to make every choice. Most were my most dangerous and painful times. God protects babies and fools. I was a fool, thinking I was fooling life, only to be fooled. My mom and son have an excellent relationship, thanks to her. She helped raise my son when I was drinking and even when I wasn't, she was right there. I used to drink so much I would have alcohol poisoning and just sleep it through until I felt better, then I was back at it. I had dreams and felt I was going to die if I didn't get a handle on my drinking. I tried it all—coolers, wine, and beer. It was never enough. *Never!*

April 24, 2019

Wednesday was just another day. Well, at least that's what I thought. Around 1:30 p.m. as I prepared for school, it was finals. I was super excited that I had another semester behind me. I had to do presentations back to back. I smoked at least two cigarettes because my nerves were all over the place. Rushing toward the metro, I felt a little off balance thinking maybe I needed to slow down. As I was coming down the escalator, I started to feel dizzy, lightheaded, nauseous, and my heart started pounding very fast. I made it down and decided to sit for a second to get myself together, and a random lady noticed me and helped as I passed out for a few seconds, maybe a minute. As I came to, I drank a little water. I didn't feel the need to go to the hospital. I figured the panic attack all came from my workload, school, and personal life. I walked back to my job because I knew I wouldn't make it to school, but I was troubled because today was finals. My co-workers didn't know what was going on, and I didn't want to tell them either. I told them my teachers canceled class just to buy time as to why I'm not heading to school for finals. Not that I didn't trust them, but I knew if I said more, I would be on my way to the hospital. I called my mother, letting her know what happened. She felt the same way: I might be overdoing it that I needed to rest. I stayed up late doing last-minute projects and showing my dedication to a dead-end relationship. My mother met me at the corner near my job. We went back down the metro, and my anxiety raised again, but I got through it. I cried inside because I knew I pushed myself a little more than usual, but this usual was different, and I wasn't okay. Once home, I had no appetite. I decided to take a hot shower and go straight to sleep.

April 25, 2019

The game changer. I woke up Thursday morning, not sure about my own body. I was dressed by 8:10 a.m., ready to see my primary care doctor. I called and asked if they were taking walk-ins today. They agreed they would see me today. Someone just canceled their appointment. On my way, I smoked two to three cigarettes for a ten-minute ride. Of course, I was nervous and shaky throughout my whole body because somehow my brain couldn't convince my heart that everything was okay. I knew I was exhausted, but I couldn't explain the uncertainty that I didn't need to see someone about what's going on. It was like God himself was whispering in my ear to go see what's happening. Those are the signs we pray for, so why not listen. Even when I wanted to back out and diagnose myself, God put one foot in front of the other. Finally, I was in my doctor's office, telling her everything I experienced the prior day. During my exam with her, I couldn't walk a straight-line heel-to-toe without losing my balance or feeling fatigue. She also wanted to do an EKG. When I laid back, her assistant asked me if I were nervous or cold because you could literally see my heart beating through my chest. I wasn't nervous anymore; I was sure something was on the rise. After minutes of waiting on my results, her assistant walked through the door with referrals to go see a few other specialists. I started to feel a sense of relief, but then my primary care physician walked in and suggested that I go to the emergency room immediately! She saw some things on my EKG that highly alerted her. I sat on the table for an additional five minutes, hoping that when stepped down my legs don't collapse. Coming to tell my mother and sister my heart was in the bottom of my shoes that I needed to go to the hospital now. My mother suggested the Hospital of Hearts, which they're known for, especially when it comes to matters of the heart. During another short but seemingly long ride, I again smoked about four cigarettes and calling my then boyfriend to get some sense of support about going to the emergency room abruptly. After telling him what's going on, I only got an "Oh, okay," as if I told him I scraped my knee. I quickly prompted myself to do this alone. I even tried persuading myself he would come after work. Nope! Another day of realizing people aren't built like me. A sense of urgency to me isn't the same for other people. Arriving at the emergency room, you must stand in line and tell them what's wrong. I must have had this strong empowered look on my face because my energy was at zero, but I stood. Even standing there, I wanted to pass out because I felt dizzy and off track. With walking, it felt like something so impossible to do. Not that it hurt, but it just seemed like it took so much energy. Once I got registered, I was called back within thirty minutes. Another EKG was done as the doctor had the same facial reaction as my primary care doctor. Without many words, exhaustion was no longer the issue. Hour after hour waiting to see a doctor, they finally arrived, only to tell me that I'll be staying overnight for observations. Now, on movies when your doctor says that you'll stay overnight for observations and they come to your room the next day, they tell you to take it easy for a couple of days. Whew! Maybe exhaustion was the problem, and rest would cure everything. A nurse came in and told me that I was being admitted to the hospital and the doctor ordered for me to have an echocardiogram sonogram done. She proceeded to ask me if it's okay to insert another IV for more testing. That's where they basically take pictures of your heart from the outside. The process is merely easy and can be done in the emergency room next to the bed. In comes this foreign doctor. Sounds familiar? He throws the curtains back intensely and says, "I'm here to do your echocardiogram." As he places the gel on my chest, every other sound was *mmmm*. He was rather aggressive, but I thought he had to do it like that to get the pictures. I already hated it here. I was told that I would be going upstairs to a more comfortable bed and room. My mother and I stayed in the emergency room from 1:15 p.m. Thursday afternoon until Friday 9:30 p.m., where we constantly froze because we asked for more covers the entire night. Now upstairs I must admit I met some cool nurses, awesome assistants, and students. It was this one student named, well, let's just call her Ebony. I know she'll be a great doctor one day for sure. She saw the fear in my eyes a mile away, not to mention the millions of questions I asked and had. Okay, let's be honest, I knew something wasn't right, but I needed a cigarette. She was one of many students who were studying medicine. I started getting extra IVs in my arm for more testing and blood drawn damn near every other hour. Being a potential cardiac patient can be very difficult especially if it's something new.

April 26, 2019

Friday, I had a doctor come by and ask me if it were okay if a few students could come pass and listen to my heartbeat. I agreed because I'm all for students becoming doctors and bettering their experience. What he didn't explain that it'll be ten to thirteen students gang-raping my heart. I felt so uncomfortable after the third person, but the stethoscope went around so fast, I couldn't tell you where the line begun or ended. They introduce themselves, but it was no meet-and-greet. I never saw them again except for one young lady Ms. Ebony. She came and talked to me every day and checked in on me without being asked. She did things for me outside her studies, but that too makes a great doctor. Her bedside manners were exceptional. My nurses stayed up with me all night explaining all the new ways technology in medicine has changed. They were very impressed and moved. As for me, I sat there bug-eyed, hoping I didn't need any of this shit.

April 27, 2019

I got the news that my echocardiogram sonogram showed blood leaking from my heart and the results from the echocardiogram wasn't as clear as they wanted. I never thought too much into it because I know a lot of people with heart murmurs. So now here I am waiting for them to tell me I needed that horrifying TEE procedure done that the nurses were talking about. TEE or transesophageal echocardiogram is done by numbing the back of your throat with this awful tasting spray, but usually smells like bananas. Sedation is given to make you feel as comfortable as possible. I'll never forget this day. The tech doing my TEE said before we began the procedure, "I don't know why no one has told you, but you're going to need heart surgery. This is a major problem." The tears and shock instantly hit my whole body. I could not stop crying because this wasn't what I thought was going on. I seriously thought I would need some medicine at the most, but *surgery*! The doctors were as supportive as they knew how to be, considering the news they dropped on me. That was the first time anyone even mentioned surgery, yet alone heart surgery. As the procedure had to go on, I was no longer sedated. I just lay there as they pulled the cord back and forth to get pictures from the inside. The results came back, and there was worse news. My heart valves weren't just a small problem. They were completely damaged. I spent the rest of the night crying because I knew life would be different hereafter. I cried for fear, struggle, my son, my addiction, and possibilities of death. I don't want to sound arrogant, but the same voice I heard telling me to go to doctor and pushing me, is the same voice every day telling me I will not die, but I must do something different and new. "I lent you time on this earth, and I lent you this body. We will rebuild and start fresh." I always wondered what my purpose is on this earth. I didn't realize God was literally sitting me down to discuss his plan. You noticed how I said his plan. Every day it's been God, Jesus, my mother, and me. I felt lonely at first, but after naming my crew, I guess it's not so bad. Worldly people have worldly thing to do. I'm not upset with anyone. Okay, I'm a little crushed. I really thought some people close to me would have showed up more. I have a few great friends who I can truly count on. My family is awesome and has been my rock before this even happened. So many laughs. I can't count how many blessings has crossed my path through this time. God has sent me plenty of angels.

April 28, 2019

Wasn't an awful day but not great. The worst part of all of this was knowing I had a boyfriend, and he was nowhere to be found. When I told him I was going to the emergency room, he didn't even flinch. I was in the hospital four days before he decided to come visit. Thank God for parking because he probably wouldn't show up after that. He gave me the excuse that he had to work, and his rent was due. If you ever wondered what broken-hearted looked from the outside in, I was lying down in a hospital recapping my entire life. So regardless, twenty minutes out of your day to see your supposed-to-be woman who had been in the hospital never crossed your mind. He told me his plans about working, driving for money and rent, and he had to do what's best for him, because if he can't pay his rent, he has no one, but that's no excuse why I wasn't a part of the daily plans. I would have never let him be alone. Not one day, but I guess it tells you the truth. When a man truly loves you, it's not about what he does; it's about what he sacrifices for you. Let's just say I'm still on the market. How dare he say, "I think we should just be friends" in the midst of my tears and the hardship news at this point because he keeps letting me down. I cried because I couldn't believe someone would do that, but a sense of relief came to me as well. I didn't have to pretend to be strong anymore. He sat down and told me all this foolery, how his dad never did women right, and his aunt said he's just like his dad in so many ways. If the stories are true, then absolutely. He had never been in a real relationship, and he's doing the best he knows how. Bullshit, at almost forty years old, he should know something. Truth of the matter, he is doing the best he can for him, not us. I should have listened when he told me had trust issues. I've been paying my dues to men for the trust they lost from women before me and that can't blink a moment of my life. However, my sister girl and my beautiful young ladies came to see me, which melted my already damaged heart. Of course, in a good way my niece is so lucky to have such great friends. She'll understand once she's older. Their visit meant the world to me. Please don't be fooled that I never mentioned my son. We talk every day, but I try to understand from his point of view, and I get it—no pressure at all. I know this is hard to accept and deal with, so I take small steps on how he wants to interact.

April 29, 2019

I had two god-awful IVs in my arm. One was put in very painful, the other because I needed so many procedures, and medication needed to go through the IVs. I see many patients come and go from my room, but this one old-ass couple drove me crazy. The roommates I had was a woman who consistently bossed her husband around. I don't think necessarily he was a punk; it was genuine love. She kept complaining it was hot in the room. Instead of asking for help, he took it upon himself. Messing with the thermometer, he ripped the cover off and something like air sounded off. I say air because I didn't smell like gas. Long story short, after Tuesday and having great news that I could leave the hospital until my surgery made my day.

April 30, 2019

I finally got to go home. It was weird because they said I needed emergency surgery within a week, but they were sending me home sooner than needed. They didn't take my insurance at that time. They sent me home with a to-do manual and a heart monitor to check my heart in the meantime. My mother ordered a ride. Crazy and amazing thing, my driver had the same open-heart surgery. He told me I'll get through it. "Just pray and let God do his thing. You got this!" he said as we high-fived. When I arrived home at 5 or 6 o'clock in the evening, I was anticipating seeing my son, which was all that mattered. He walked through the door, dropped everything, cried, and hugged me like never in life. In that very moment, I realized my son needed me more than ever. The feeling was so mutual. We've always had a unique bond. Most people say we're very close like brother and sister, but he knows I'm his mother—nothing more and certainly nothing less. I rest the remaining Tuesday and caught up on some shows I've missed with my stay in the hospital.

May 1, 2019

Wednesday, I felt better than ever. I was up, out of bed, finally breathing in the fresh air. Store runs and enjoying life as I know it. Still continuing to catch up on shows. Put in for a leave of absence at my job. Still helping my team with things that they needed as much as I can. Most people told me, "Don't worry about work," but I had to make sure things were done properly. I was nervous if I didn't help, I would lose my job and wouldn't be able to return. I hated the thought of not supporting myself and my son.

May 2, 2019

Was all about eating what I wanted and relaxing. Took a car ride, which I enjoyed because the scenery of everything makes me happy. Went to Giant to get my nicotine gum. I've quit smoking cigarettes cold turkey. Literally running around waiting for the pharmacy to get the prescription filled was a headache itself. One more day then my cravings will be helped. I finally mustered up the courage to tell my closest friends what's been going on with me. When I first found out, it was the birthday of one of my best friends, and here I was in the hospital trying to put the pieces back together. One of my best friends reached out and told me how much it hurt her that I was having heart surgery. I know she's sensitive just like me. So I can only imagine how that made her feel.

May 3, 2019

It's payday finally; I can go get my hair done and take these raggedy nails off. Went to ride with my uncle to drop my son off at school. Drinking my golden brown (coffee), which is delicious—he makes it for me each morning. I'm drinking my coffee feeling fine, but it was the 7-11 store run that things started to change. I started wondering if the lady who called me a thousand times knew they shouldn't have released me from the hospital, because they didn't take my insurance but knew I needed that surgery soon as possible. It was scary because she wanted me to lie and say I'm having chest pain and come back through the emergency room. I was still shocked from the news. Anyway, I got a cup of coffee for my mother, got in line, and started to feel fatigue and lightheaded again. I immediately put the cup down and walked out the store. My uncle asked if I was okay. I wasn't but I started taking deep breaths and trying to relax myself. I couldn't allow myself to faint or be in an unfamiliar space. I just needed to be in the presence of my mother. My brother wanted to take me to Great Falls to enjoy the views. I haven't been since I was a little girl. Unfortunately, my body wasn't up for it. I constantly called on Jesus. Naturally being nervous, I knew I was okay. I just needed to feel secure. My mother asked if I wanted to go or stay home. I told her I'll stay behind. My body wasn't up to do much. Never doubting myself or going against my special voice, I decided to go to the emergency room, which again turned into the best choice except here was a little different. They moved fast. There was no long waiting to see a doctor or get a room in the back. The process of the emergency room was nothing new for me. This hospital had technology that worked and moved a little faster for results. Once settled, doctors and discussions were made, which I respected because I like that they got other opinions. Around 10:30 p.m. I had another echocardiogram done, but this time the lady was very gentle and talked to me, instead of throwing around a monitor on my chest with cold gel and processing as if I didn't matter and wanted it to be over quickly.

May 4, 2019

Saturday morning, I was woken to my normal routine. Checking vital signs and blood drawings. A CT scan was on my board for the plan of care. My transporter was at the room at 5:30 a.m. I'm here for it! I wonder, do the hospital and psychologists work together because all the transporters were very nice-looking men and women. I've never felt uncomfortable in the presence of them. Just curious if that's a strategy used by hospitals. The CT scan is something unbelievable. It gives your doctor very clear images, and they inject you with this dye that's cold at first then hot as hell. The sensation makes you feel like you urinated on yourself but didn't. The look of the machine is intimidating but only takes literally five minutes to do. I'm taken back to my room, ready for breakfast and waiting on the next move plus results. I already knew what I was facing because things were similar as they were in the other hospital. They said doctors don't do rounds on weekends. Don't believe the hype. I saw my doctor on a Sunday. She explained exactly what she saw on my results on the previous test/procedure. It's finally clear that I'll need open-heart surgery, but she explained some things that the other hospital didn't even acknowledge. I'm not trusting her. I'm trusting God with her. I trust the process. I have no choice because I'm living through it every day. I've had very bad days where tears were my only visitors. Then great days. I have nurses who wasn't on my team come visit me. People from the emergency room even stopped past. There were caregivers who assisted a woman in my room who prayed for me and with me. Hugs were my new best friends. Numerous texts from very close friends, sisters, and co-workers. I didn't expect an abundant of calls and texts because I kept this very private. I knew I needed my strength and telling this story again would break me down. I had to completely numb myself from the inside out. My known squad is truly reliable. I've watched visitors come and go for others. I never once got jealous because I looked at their situations and see that their needs are mostly dependent on others. Even though loneliness occurs from time to time, I know this is my time with the Lord alone. To talk, pray, forgive, and humble myself through everything here and later. I'm forever grateful that my doctor paid enough attention to me and listened. I'm grateful that God has allow me this to get ideas rolling. I've been a procrastinator since the day I was born. I feel it deep down in my soul, God has chosen this time for me and him. I'm honored to be a witness to how God speaks to us. I've spent days trying to figure out how I was going to cope, deal, or express myself through this. I never bother thinking about the true recovery. I was thinking about how I'll never pick a cigarette or bottle up again. How things will need to be addressed without an addiction to depend on. I know my number one supporter knows everything beforehand. I didn't bother praying for clarity. I wanted to know how I was going to get through the rest of my life sober. Here I was nearly dying, and my only thought was a cigarette and alcohol. Then, the idea of a journal through this journey would be nice. Maybe a book. Not the journey of the open-heart surgery, but how I got through this time without drinking or smoking. It's not often a woman from Southwest Washington, DC, gets to tell her story of an unexpected life-changing experience to the world. The thought of how, where, when, and who would publish this started to consume me. But then I realized I'm not trusting the process because this is only the beginning. It's not easy, but I can't decide something unfinished. I continue to let God lead my hand and heart every day.

May 6, 2019

Woke up with a board full of plans. EC TEE, cath lab, and MRI cardiac. Of course, I was a little fussy about doing these things because I've been through one of these procedures before, not my best memory. Well, I tried to do the MRI cardiac, but I couldn't do it. The nurse gave me a Xanax, but it did nothing for me. I went down there feeling hopeful, but I couldn't do it, especially after she told me it would take one to two hours to get pictures. I completely lost it. Nope, this will not be done today. I was a crying mess. The only thing that made me feel better was seeing my mother's face coming through the door. God, what would I do without her? She's my true best friend. There's nothing in this entire world she can't have once I get it. I owe her beyond belief. She's not only here for me, but she also continuously takes care of my son. After all my bullshit, how can I be so lucky. It truly feels good to be cigarette and alcohol free for the moment. It's time to live life. I felt bad because I was trying to be understanding of everything. I know my mission is here and now for a reason, and God is going to carry me through. I was saying forgiving, but I need to be asking for forgiveness myself. Lord, I pray you forgive me for all my sins. Lord, I ask that when I'm weak, you give me strength and most of all when I cry, you cleanse my soul to make room for the truth in me. I pray I will own and love who I will become. I see that it's my time to truly stand on faith. I've been through some things, but this time God is speaking directly to me. I'm listening and I know great things are coming. I must say I'm happily nervous to make the moves, but I'm sick and tired of being where I've been. This is my story and I'm not settling for simple when God's love is unconditional. I'm going to read tonight and watch a little television, just relax as much as I can. In Jesus' name I pray. Amen.

May 7, 2019

Tuesday was full of events. Here, I am ready to get my EC TEE and cath lab done. It's refreshing to see they have a window in here. Lord, I haven't been outside in a while. I cherish everything I see—the trees, dirt, grass, buildings, cars, and the people walking about. How dare I take these things for granted. How blessed am I. Lord, I pray everything goes well. They got the pictures they need because that cardiac MRI will be missing me today. Everything went okay, thank you, Jesus. I requested some sedative medicine because they wanted me to do a CAT scan. The CAT scan wasn't bad at all. I came back to my room to get a Facetime session with my favorite friend—got to love him. He's a great co-worker who helped me a lot. After a few good laughs and jokes, my mother walked in, which always makes me super happy. She's so supportive and knows exactly what to say to keep me calm and focused. She my favorite part of every day. Then an old special friend walks through the door. I can't lie. I was excited he showed up and not that he would lie, but it was nice that he came through to see me. I never really understood where we stood in our relationship. It was always clear we were more than friends, but never exclusive. I craved him in a different way. He gave me what he had, and I need more. Hell, I wanted more than his fancy extensive vocabulary. I've probably seen the real him twice and desired that ever since. I was mad as hell the hospital didn't get my food in time, but thanks to one of my favorite nurses, she got me something to eat. Finally, feeling like I accomplished everything on my end leading up to surgery. I thought I was going to relax on Wednesday and try to focus on the great things to come after surgery. Like breathing better, exercising, and eat healthy. Focusing on life in any way possible, not being afraid to take risks. Heart surgery is a risk, and I'm all in for the Lord to do his work. I can't eat nothing after midnight. I'm scared as hell. Sometimes, I think I have all the information needed, then something else comes up. I've never experienced anything like this in my life. I'm happy my doctor will be performing my surgery; I know I'll be okay. I just can't seem to shake these anticipation bugs. I know I'm supposed to be a trooper. Trooper is a family saying we use to keep the positive energy. I cried every night, and every night seemed lonely. The nighttime always let me know that even with all those visitors, this is something you must face and deal with alone. This is only something you get through when you have no choice. And God tells you to man up. I walk by blind faith. My process shows every day. Thank you, Lord, for another day. Forever grateful.

May 8, 2019

I watched the clock tick every second. Waking up to call for breakfast seemed hard because minutes went by fast. I had so many visitors today, which helped calm my nerves, but never enough to take eyes off the clock. My cousin brought me flowers. We've been for each other since we were kids. He'll always have my heart. Blood bonded. That guy—my now ex-boyfriend. Mr. We-Should-Be-Friends I told you about—came to the hospital empty-handed again after days. So embarrassing. I guess I was supposed to appreciate his efforts, but I wasn't convinced at all. However, I didn't have time to focus on his mistakes or faults. We didn't talk much, honestly, but truthfully, I'm glad we didn't. I was too broken to let another situation sit on my heart. I've never spoke aloud about this, but I felt abandoned by my sister. As the night fell, I became very antsy and nervous. The cardiac surgery came to see me, ordered me some Benadryl because I was having stress hives, and it helped with my sleeping. My mother and brother were my last visitors tonight. I was scared shitless because I was still waiting for all those doctors to come in my room and say, "It's a miracle! You don't need surgery." That never happened. My nurse that night told me to just relax and he'll do everything else. I remembered my surgeon telling me to shower the night before and the next morning. I ended up not showering because my nurse said I didn't have to be up until 6:30 a.m. I talked to mother that night until I was sure I was calm. My aunt called me. That night we talked for hours. She told me everything will be fine. She is sending my uncle and cousin, who I call my brother, over to see me until they release her from the hospital tomorrow. I was so afraid but secured at the same time, if that makes sense. Usually, my aunt would tell me to buckle up and take the ride with whatever comes, but this night she let me talk until I had nothing else to say. I cried and laughed. My last conversation was with her and God asking him to heal and protect every hand involved with my surgery.

May 9, 2019

12:00 midnight approached. Today is the day. I literally woke up every hour on the hour, counting how much time I had left before it was time for surgery. I was woken up to a nurse who I didn't recognize say I have fifteen minutes before they come get me and take me to pre-op. It's 5:45 a.m. and I'm confused about why I'm up so early. Not to mention I'm on my cycle, a woman's worst nightmare with any situation. I had to wipe down with these surgical wipes and then off I go. I heard nurses were upset because my nurse for the night was on a cigarette break, when I supposed to be up and ready waiting on transportation to pre-op. The ride there was weird because I told every nurse and doctor that I'll need something to keep me calm, because I don't believe I will make it without it. Somehow, I was very silent and calm. I heard nothing or moved. It was like my body was temporarily numb and paralyzed. Now in the pre-operation waiting room, I see my name first on the board for surgery, which is refreshing and nerve-racking. One because I'm first and people are normally refreshed in the morning, and the nerve-racking part, will I be their first mistake of the day? I finally see the anesthesiologist and how I got a few questions I forgot, plus more. She reassured me that everything will be okay, and her mom went through the surgery and she's doing great. My surgeon walked in and made me super comfortable before surgery. She answered every concern and doubt. Because they couldn't hide my mom. She filled in and gave me the biggest hug ever. Now, it's time to go into the surgery room. The halls are bright and cold. As I entered my operating room, it was beautifully designed. I was introduced to everyone on the team. If that don't you make you feel confident, I'm not sure what does for open-heart surgery. They had a huge monitor on with a playlist. They put my mask on and asked what song would I like to hear. Without hesitation, "I Was Here," by one of my favorite performers. She is dope as fuck. Once I was asleep, the surgery took seven hours. I have no idea what life was afterward. All I remember is Friday waking up completely.

May 10, 2019

Waking up to a breathing tube, which drove me crazy until my doctors decided to pull it. I coughed briefly, but that was it. I sipped water the whole time. I was so dehydrated. No water or food since Wednesday night. I was taking baby breaths all day; I was scared to take a deep breath because I thought I would bust my chest open. My nurses in ICU were awesome. When I had to move from the bed to the chair, I know I had to, but that shit was torture. I vividly remember them telling me, "It's time to move around," but the first move is the hardest move. They weren't lying either. I felt like I was going to die. It was painful. I had to look up at the ceiling so I wouldn't faint, but I was happy to be out of the bed. Back in bed hours later, reflecting on how I ended here but glad and thankful to be alive. My mother finally brought me my cellphone. My cousin called me saying my aunt just went into cardiac arrest and now she's on a breathing machine. I was so confused because I talked to her Wednesday night and everything seemed fine. We talked about how she'll help and listen to me every day about how I feel or what aches and pains I'm going to have with recovery. My cousin must have pocket dialed me. I heard everything before he originally called me back. My cousin called me an hour later and said, "She gone. Ma gone Tu she died." I was barely breathing myself. Taking in that kind of news, I was so devastated. I was crushed. I'm not even through twenty-four hours out of heart surgery and to receive this news, I didn't know what to do. My soul shook in a different way. My nurses asked how I was doing because my blood pressure kept raising. I said fine because I knew if I would have said it aloud, I would've fallen apart. I knew I needed to live because I instantly thought about my son, mother, my sisters, and brothers. I couldn't die. I need to live. I must live and I want to live. For the first time in my life, I was pissed with God. I couldn't believe he took my aunt away from me, but in the same breath I was confused to why he chose me to live. Not that it's a competition, but I understood my aunt's job here on earth was completed, while I had more work to do. Suddenly, I stopped questioning the situation. I was numb to everything. I was confused and angry. Why did I have to go through this? I started naming so many other people who I thought were deserving of such painful surgery or death. Then I recognized after thinking why I was here in the first place. Was God giving me a second chance at life to rid all the harmful things I did to my body, mind, heart, and soul. To right my wrongs for the damage I caused to other people. I didn't cry because I was in shock. My best friend came to see me. I was excited because it was a face I recognized after surgery. My mother showed up later. They had a physical therapist come show me some techniques about getting back on my feet again. I really liked them, so I tried as much as I could at the time. The next time one came. I was so rude and wasn't willing to try because I wasn't in the mood. I wanted to hate God. How could he punish me like this again? Besides, my aunt was on my mind. I just kept waiting for her to walk through the door. Reality won't settle in. This felt like some weak-ass Lifetime movie shit. *It's not real!*

May 11, 2019

Today was a shitty day. I really didn't want much but my aunt to walk through the door. I ate food so nobody would bug me about not eating. My doctors finally took out the large IV in my neck. I felt so relieved because I could move my neck in peace and with ease. I literally stayed in bed that day. I wondered how my uncle Dawson was holding up. My brother and my sister was on another continent in Asia on her way home. My body felt like I was trapped inside somewhere I had no place being. I kept reasoning with myself that this was a blessing, and I was getting restored, but honestly, I felt like it was my turn to endure the worst pain ever. Through all the anger, frustration, confusion, and sadness, deep down inside I was walking on this magic faith and had the same feeling when I was a little girl. I felt something in my heart that gave me confirmation that there's a God. This process I had the same feeling, but I looked at the circumstances differently this time around. I started naming all wonderful things I've done in life, as if I was giving God my confirmation to live. Then I started thinking about all the shitty things I did as well. Is this my biggest karma yet? Today wasn't a good day at all. I did everything the nurses told me to do, so I didn't have to hear anyone's mouth. I want to break down, but I couldn't seem to let go of anything. I watched TV as if I cared about anything that was on. Worst day ever. Tears felt like first cousins. Oh well.

May 12, 2019

Today I was moved into my own room upside. I was finally out of ICU. Today was one of the best and emotional days. My whole family came to see me. My brother from Shawful and his family, which put the biggest smile on my face. I was extremely happy to see my uncle Dawson because I know he was crushed to his soul about my aunt. We talked every day about plans with my aunt and how he would be done with dating, but who knew. It was the painful cries in his eyes. It took everything in me to fight every tear back. I looked over at my oldest brother and I'll be damned, I saw the lost soul, a little boy whose mom left without warning. Not out the door, but off this earth to her real home. My sister hung around longer than anyone. I knew she wanted a moment alone, but she looked like she was holding it all together. I saw right through it all, but I didn't want to speak on anything she wasn't ready to speak on. It was like my twin came through to see me. I couldn't sleep until I saw her face. I needed her and I knew she needed me. We'd been at each other's side since the crib. There's no breaking this bond. Today was a better day. Family is everything to me. Not to mention my best friend from elementary school—twenty-three years of friendship—came through to see me. I knew when I told her she would understand. Not that she had the surgery, but that's her field. She knew exactly what I was talking about when I spoke on my situation about needing open-heart surgery. She's sensitive just like me. I love my sister forever. Her visit meant the world to me. As night settled in, I started to realize what was important in life. Tears fell endlessly because they were tears of joy because I made it through and overwhelmed with sadness because my aunt wasn't here to witness that I made it through. From day one, we talked every day about what to expect and how I felt. She fried me chicken every day. I still can't accept what's real. We had plans. Why did you leave? Cardiac floor has some of the best nurses ever! I truly appreciate all of them for taking care of me. I know nurses are supposed to have some type of detachment because of patients, but they all left a mark on my heart. I wish I could name them all officially, but I'm sure they know who they are. Best nurses crew of all time. I'm sure I'm biased, but I survived with them.

May 13, 2019

Woke to Ms. Mallory ready to walk and do our daily routine. She was a Jamaican lady with a heart of gold and a spirit that makes you smile when you were angry. She also made you work hard to heal yourself back to health. No excuse ever worked with her. Except there were days I didn't need to say anything, and she would let me lie in bed and cater to my every need. I wonder if she knew. Honestly, I'm happy she's my nurse for the day because I knew my mind would be busy and focused on getting better. The thoughts of my aunt couldn't consume me. I knew the doctor fixed my heart, but I can confirm my heart was still hurting due to emotional pain. I was getting all the medicine and physical therapy as needed. They rarely discuss the aftermath of surgery like patients feeling depressed, sad, or lost. I felt every emotion possible after surgery. The doctors are supposed to physically fix the problem, which they did, but you can never be prepared for depression, PSTD, and anxiety. Most times I spent crying because I didn't recognize myself. The person in the mirror was now a stranger too. Of course, I had my memories, but as far as this person, who used to be somewhat healthy to the eye, is now damaged goods. My family, friends, doctors, and nurses all tell me how brave I am, but I wonder if my countless tears counted as bravery too. My other aunt and cousin came to visit. I needed that because the tears were way too much for me. They kept me very entertained. My best friend, well, I should say, sister came to end my night—the best. I hated that she had to leave, but I knew she had to go. I wanted to break down and let everything go, but my pride won't allow my vulnerability to lead my emotions. I was back watching TV, thinking how I'm supposed to bounce back from this. Sleep was my energy; it just didn't come easy or at all.

May 14, 2019

I woke up and did my early morning walk, twice around the hospital wing. Ate a good breakfast and Lord, behold my cousin and aunt walked through the door. We laughed and joked for hours. My heart was with much joy. Today was filled with mixed emotions. I didn't know what I wanted to do. Cry, yell, die, or survive. Sometimes during the day, I felt the worst pain anyone can endure. Most times I never said anything because I felt like I deserved to be in pain. I started thinking about all the shit I did and honoring the pain because I felt if I got past it, then I'm paying my dues of the things I did. My aunt's sudden death affected me tremendously. I'm sure my family felt the pain. I just felt so alone and not close enough to my family. I felt guilty. I had survivor's guilt because I felt like my family had to choose between staying home and mourn my aunt or come visit me and pretend to hide the dry tears and fight back any potential memories that provoked new ones. I hated being here. I hated death even though I know it will eventually happen, but damn, I hated that we both didn't survive. I was sick to my stomach; the thought wouldn't escape me. Why me? I know we're not supposed to question God's work because he makes no mistake, but how much can one person take. I know God never put more than we can bear. I must be the new superwoman because I wasn't ready or this strong. Well,

God clearly said otherwise because I'm here, but let me be the first to say this shit isn't easy. I want someone to talk to but can't seem to let my mother out of my sight for too long. I don't trust anyone with me unfamiliar. This whole experience in and out the hospital. I did nothing without my mother next to me. She has MS or multiple sclerosis, and she devoted her energy and time to me. My cardiac surgery assistant came in with the news that I might go tomorrow. I was anxious and worried. I wanted to go home because I missed my family, but I was nervous because I am nearing a journey on my own. The doctors and nurses will no longer be my shoulder. My mother will have my back for sure, but I knew she would let go of my hand and push me a little. I was once again scared shitless because a new beginning was around the corner.

May 15, 2019

Here I was waiting on my bloodwork and the words that I could go home. Well, unfortunately, I couldn't go home just yet because my blood levels weren't high enough. I had one nurse who I liked, but I didn't give her the respect she deserved. She was super dope and treated me great. So I decided to give her a good walk around the floor and have conversation. When nighttime came and the nurses switched shifts, I was a little disappointed I didn't give her more time and efforts on my part. I had these young ladies who were my new nurses. I thought at first they didn't know what they were doing, but I must say they were just as good as any other. They were sweet, but they pushed me out of bed too. I wasn't allowed to be lazy and give useless excuses. They played their part and I owed mine as well. They earned my respect as it was well deserved. Let's say I was happy when their shift was over. This one male nurse I've seen around the floor wing sometimes ended up being my nurse. He was always rushing and moving too damn fast for me. I was introduced to him and I went to sleep, hopefully wondering what tomorrow will bring. I want to go home.

May 16, 2019

Here's the day I was waiting for patiently. Every time someone neared my door, I thought it would be one of the cardiac surgeons telling me the good news I might go home today. Dreams do come true. Here come one of them now. Her face had great news versus yesterday when I couldn't leave. I was finally granted the opportunity to leave the hospital. After removing the tubes and wires, which were unexpectedly painful and some easier than I thought, I somewhat felt a little human. My male nurse gave me the rundown of the do's and don'ts. One instruction he gave scared me about going to the ocean and my chest busting open because my stitches won't hold. Let's get the hell out of here. I was so happy to be home. My house smelt different, no more cigarette smoke. I sat on the couch and took it all in. I was so grateful to be among my family. I still felt afraid because I was so used to the hospital and the nurses. I didn't know what to do. I knew my mom would help me, but I knew I would eventually have to let her hand go. I kept looking around waiting for something to be out of place. I wanted to adjust to something different because that Wednesday I left for work and school. The house was the same, very clean. Feeling so uptight because I still haven't processed that I had open-heart surgery or my aunt's death. I was living outside my body until warranted tears fell from my eyes. I walked past the mirrors for the first time in weeks and I recognized myself in full fresh, but this wasn't me. This is not my life; I didn't spend a month in the hospital being broken down to my core. I literally know what it means to be stripped down to my soul completely naked, nothing to hide. Any and every emotion exposed was my new life. I needed help with everything I did. I barely cough without assistance. It was a delivery at the door from a friend. Sent me some delicious fruit and it put a smile on my face. I was overwhelmed. I played my heart not to think about my aunt's sudden death the very next day after my surgery. Honestly, I didn't feel like was going to make it myself after surgery the way I was breathing, but I made a strong choice and prayed to God to let me live. I prayed for every breath I took.

Nothing came easy, not even the air we so easily take for granted. I just wanted another day behind me.

May 17, 2019

What a day! I woke up crying because I was in pain. This is not my body. How do I get used to this? What do I do now? How do I live? I have no idea; I just keep getting up putting one foot in front of the other. I know you're thinking how I can be so ungrateful when you're alive and breathing. Here I am questioning every move and breath I take. How do you manage a new heart and feel sad, angry, confused, and broken all at the same time? I cried every hour on the hour. I hated that I was unable to be who I thought I was supposed to be. I understand God makes decisions and plans for our lives for the best. I'm still unwilling to accept what it is at this point. It didn't matter how hurt or angry I was. My life is forever different. My emotions continued to ride a roller coaster. One minute, I felt happy to be alive, and the very next I lay up useless and helpless, trying to discover this hidden secret woman I am supposed to be. But she cried endlessly because she too was lost for words. Dear God, thank you for allowing me this opportunity to a new life. I didn't forget about those promises I made to you. I plan on going through with all of them, but in the meantime please excuse my bullshit. I thought the surgery was my nightmare. Damn! The recovery is kicking my ass. The depression, anxiety, sadness, frustration, confusion, and anger can really tear your body down. Everyone says how brave I was. It was only God—I will not take the credit on this one. Every second that passed I kept thinking how you keep someone alive with a broken heart from love, a crushed soul from my loved one. It was purpose. I had family who needed me alive. Besides, I know God is using me to open a door that's only designed for me. I must be open to accept this challenge. I hear God talking every day. We discussed everything. I see the world differently each time I open my eyes. It's always a new flower or how the sun is angled the next day. I usually come up with amazing ideas, but I never complete them, well, hell, I don't even start the idea. God has been moving my pen and thoughts on paper. It's been days. I didn't like writing or felt like I didn't want to share shit. I needed to cry and ball up in the corner, except my chest couldn't take the extra drama I wanted to display. I thought writing about my journey with open-heart surgery would be dope, but it took a new turn in an unexpected direction. I'm telling my story of how I spent more than a month in the hospital and come home, only to fall apart. No place was comfortable to me except seeing my mother close by was my only sanity.

May 18, 2019

Another day of bullshit and tears. My day was full of pretending I was okay. My sister came to see me. I was happy to see her. But I wondered, Did my mother ask her to come. I was confused why she wasn't here as much as she was for other people. I was not mad. I was hurt that she wasn't present. I was reminded of my aunt. We didn't discuss her at all. We casually talked about it as if neither one of us wanted to deal with it head on. Honestly, my healing is so hard to do with my aunt's death so close to everything that's been going on. I've been saying I need someone to talk to professionally because I'm so lost. Do I yell, cry, or focus on myself? I know my aunt would want me to move on because she's no longer with us in the flesh. My heart has had a replacement and repaired, but I'm still so very broken. I can't come to terms that I had surgery; I still feel like this isn't my body. I know by the pain, but mentally this is not connecting at all. I wanted to talk to someone because the thoughts I have, they might think I'm crazy. I've never once thought about suicide. I love living. I'm just so fucking frustrated and removed from everything. This day was filled with sadness, tears, and misleading hope I put in my own head. Oh well! Jesus, I pray it gets better. I know it does, I'm sure this will be another time I go back and say we got through that. Thank God. Good night. My heart is overwhelmed.

May 19–20, 2019

I spent two days deciding how I want my hair because I've been wearing two cornrows in my hair for a month now. I had yellow nail that look like I was growing another set under them. My son was under me a lot those days. I never questioned it. I took every second in smelling his hair and just staring at him, as if he were growing out of my arms forever. My sister called and said she has a surprise for me. I was pressed. I couldn't wait. I love surprises, big or small. The thought always makes me feel loved. She brought me a neck pillow. That was the best surprise ever. I've been sleeping great with the pillow. Well, at least, resting my eyes. I sleep but never comfortable because sleeping on your back can really take its toll on you. Night came and I wonder why I dealt with my unnecessary pain. I've been so used to dealing with whatever cards came my way. I kept feeling like I deserved to feel the pain that took my breath away. Every thirty minutes felt like someone was stabbing me in the heart and turning the knife. I convinced myself I was supposed to go through it.

May 23–24, 2019

Three days went by as I suffered in silence. These wires in me hurt so bad, I cried mercifully to myself. I cried about everything—how lonely life feels, how much pain I was in, and my aunt. Crazy thing. I could only cry a little at a time because my cries can be strong, I didn't want to hurt myself in the process, which I was doing anyway because I sat in silence hurting every day. My mother would ask if I was okay. I said yes because all things scared me, until I couldn't take the pain anymore. Everything was a decision to be made. I went to the emergency room feeling the worst pain ever. I hated the hospital by now. Just the sight made me nauseous. I needed to be there so they could find a solution to this pain. I got admitted again, and my heart instantly dropped because I was no longer confident that things were okay. I stayed overnight because my surgeon was going to try and remove the wires so this pain would go away. I thought this was going to be an uncomplicated procedure, but after she told me the risk and said I would need to go into the operating room to do so, because there was a great risk I could bleed heavy, I quickly changed my mind. I asked for stronger medicine to go home with. Besides, it was my son's birthday today, May 24. I was sick and tired of being in the hospital. I was happy to be home for my son's birthday, even though we didn't spend much time together—typical teenagers. It was good to see his face. I know he loves me regardless.

May 25, 2019

The only thing I did was get my nails done. Thank God I feel a little normal. Oh! My toes as well. It was an okay day; I couldn't pretend what was lurking around that corner. My aunt's funeral day was getting closer and closer. My denial was at an all-time high. Denial about my recovery and my aunt's death. I battled every day what my heart can handle, but both is too much, so I pretended to be in a different place where my mind, time, and space is taken. I had good food but fuck today.

May 28, 2019

Another three days, no writing, just crying. Feeling sorry for myself. Not giving myself enough time to heal. I despise this day. I knew today would be the last day I see my aunt. Most people asked if I was going to the funeral because I still was fresh from my surgery. I had to go; today would be the day I know it's real. I could witness it for myself. My denial wouldn't let it sink in. I knew this wasn't a game, but I had to lay my own eyes on her. My second half, my best friend is officially gone from what we call earth. I also knew if I didn't go, I would've regretted it for the rest of my life. Besides, I wanted to be there for my family. Honestly, I didn't think I would've have broken down like I did. I had nothing but tears to give. She lay in peace and here I was, in pieces. I couldn't look at her too long. It's true, she'll never be here the way I wanted her. Yes, I know it's selfish, but I needed her and still do. I kept waiting for that special moment when I would really get that message from God about me being in this situation with purpose. People still tell me how brave, strong, and how amazing I am to overcome such tragedy. Truthfully, I'm shattered. I don't know how to live anymore. Everything I do consists of me not dying. The way I walk, talk, and breathe, I worry if I'm going to take my last breath. The wires inside scares the living shit out of me because I'm afraid if I move wrong, they might harm me for good. I don't want to go into the operating room ever again. Everyone in the hospital told me how young I was and how quick I would bounce back. Lies! I don't feel that at all. Besides, no one tells you that you'll bounce back from PTSD. I'm afraid as hell because I have no idea how I'm supposed to feel anymore.

May 31, 2019

My doctor's appointment is today. I'll be seeing my surgeon. I had a million questions, but when I got there, everything went away because I was supposed to happy as ever to be alive. I guess I was nervous too because my anxiety came back because all I remember is surgery and being scared to death. She said I was doing great and I look great, but inside I was dead. I was brutally being murdered by fear, anxiety, guilt, and depression. I thought about things and think I'm ready to go back to work in six weeks, but I hate my job because I was always picking my job over family, my health, and school. I'm always stressed there and honestly after the front desk, I learned everything from scratch on my own. I'm not blowing my own horn, but I've exhausted myself trying not to let people down who didn't care about me. I used the words "a lot" because there's a lot of things that I have not let go of or forgiven to be able to move on. I guess life changed so fast. I didn't get the opportunity to face anything.

It just changed. I was so sure the Lord was sitting me down to get myself together. I never knew it would cost this much. Everyone says I'll be a testimony of God's work. Of course! I believe in Jesus Christ and he's my lord and savior. I'm hopefully praying on the day I wake up with no more dizziness, lightheaded, or tightness of my chest. I've been fighting these pains and scars because I'm terrified that someone would say surgery again and my heart or soul can't bear the thought again. I'm afraid to tell my mother I'm uncomfortable because she has MS or multiple sclerosis, which she must deal with also. I'm feeling like I'm almost there at the finish line to feeling better, but I'm not grateful enough yet. Maybe because I still miss my past that was toxic. I had this vision that I needed to be stripped down to my soul to move in a different direction, but completely inside and outside to get back to that life. Trying to figure out if I needed to reconnect with unfinished business and cutting ties with long overdue unhealthy relationships that's doing nothing for my spiritual or mental growth. I heard how people moved up and on after they had done these things and became happier. Maybe, I'm still holding on to the list. I've never been afraid to meet new people, but I can be somewhat closed off. Maybe one day I'll understand.

June 2, 2019

Fuck everything. I'm just fucking over it. I look at the distance light that's so beautiful. It's something that keeps blowing out these candles and losing vision of what I saw, then I remembered. I wasn't just recovering from surgery. I was detoxing from alcohol, cigarettes, selling drugs, late nights, and early mornings. I had heart surgery. *Shit!* That hurt. Two days until we officially bury my aunt. *WTF!* I'm happy I got to talk to her that night before my surgery, but I needed her presence to walk through those doors. I know, Lord, she's yours and I thank you for allowing me to share my time with her. Maybe things wouldn't be so hard if I really gave things a chance. Instead of predicting the outcome that's not even close, I just need to live in each moment. Watching my son endlessly growing over me. Wow, things have changed before my eyes. Damn, maybe it's time to grow up, not like I'm a bum, but it's time to grow up, own my bullshit and personal shit. Become a better mother, sister, niece, friend, and daughter. A better me. I feel her pushing through, but am I ready for what I'm asking and praying about to the Lord? I wondered, if God gave me everything I prayed and asked for, would I do something with it, or I just want to escape this pain as he's always given me a temporary free pass for all my bullshit. I know things get tough before it gets better. Even with every tear, I've stayed in this moment with my faith and trust. I'm supposed to call a therapist so I can talk to someone about these feelings and emotions, but for some reason, I feel like this is God and me sessions and I need to share with him for now. Yes, I know he already planned this, but I hear his voice better every day. I know I can't be afraid to cut ties. No love lost, but I must let go of what's holding the most weight. Dreadful relationships and tempting opportunities. That's dead ends too.

June 4, 2019

Today is the day we officially lay my aunt to rest. I thought I cried all my tears, but today was just hard. It's never what you expect, nor is it the same as on television. Today totally sucked. It's crazy to have family so close, but only when tragic strikes. My family is very close as any other family would be. We're a tight family, but we're unusually close lately especially under the circumstances. I watched them lower my aunt in a vault. A part of me was taken forever too. I watched our family glue detach itself as she was put down. After her service, the family went out for food. The laughs continued, which gave my heart hope of staying close. My aunt was firm on our family, and now I clearly see why. The ride home was the hardest for me because I knew that was going to be last time I see her. My son was with us this time. I'm sure this played a major part on his heart as well. My aunt and him had a unique relationship and bond. She always fussed at him with good intentions, but he was crazy about her at the same time. I saw the tears pour down his face, and I just held his hand and let him have a moment without speaking. The remainder of the day was very quiet. No one said much, but we felt the same hurt and love all at the same time. The TV spent a whole day watching us. Today wasn't good. I'm over it all. That "God, don't put more on us than we can bear" is tough. Open-heart surgery, my closest aunt, my ace, and a broken heart. I felt like I was outside my body watching everything. This was not life, and I wasn't watching, I was dreaming, except the dreaming wouldn't end. I've looked in the mirror a thousand times. I still haven't recognized the person looking back. Outside flesh, yes, but the inside was a complete stranger. I didn't like myself. I knew I was suffering from depression, but let's not mention the outside appearances. I felt awful and looked the part, but I had to be grateful to be alive. Right? I would sound selfish as if I wanted anything more. I'll be going back to work soon, but I'm unsatisfied with my work life, but it pays the bills and I need money. I dread going back, but what else can I do. Looking for something just won't work now. Half my days are spent getting better. The other half wiping tears.

June 7, 2019

For seven days I've been putting oil/anointing myself because my mom has a friend who's a pastor that said this will heal me inside outside. My seven days are up. I'm not sure if I feel a little better because it's true or God's healing in how he does things. This experience has taught me so much about other people and myself. One, thinking about alcohol every day, but not even tempted to buy it though. I don't want to deal with the hardship of hangovers and shame, and I'm not sure what it will do to my heart. Two, cigarettes are on my mind as well. Some days I'm happy I don't smoke, but other days those were my go-to when things got crazy. My heart has been on a journey. People who I thought were so close turned out to be so distant and those who I canceled out were my biggest fans and supporters. Being stripped down and exposed about being very cold to people has struck something in me. My best friend of twenty years said she's never seen me cry, and that's true. Not because I don't have feelings, but because I never want people to see me vulnerable. I don't show emotions in relationships with men until it's too late. Most of them resurface in my life. We talk then I'll express my feelings. The same question is always asked. Why you never said anything? I promised God if he let me live, I would change my ways. I'm making good on what I said, but I still have a long way to go considering the bullshit I was up to before. I blocked so many people out of my life, but now I'm wondering if it was worth the hard grudge. I know I want to be different and do something new.

June 8, 2019

Woke up ready to get out the house, not feeling as remorseful about people in my life. Great Falls was a great place for my heart. The water was like my feelings flushing away. We walked two fall views before turning around and going to IHOP for breakfast. I really enjoyed myself with my family that morning. I consistently worried about everything I was losing. I couldn't think about what I would be gaining. I don't want to write anymore. My heart is empty yet grateful.

June 21, 2019

It been two weeks since I picked up this pen, but it wasn't because things were good. Shit, most days I prayed my way out of bed, begging God to move my soul because my heart and mind was busy shuffling emotions. I hated everything. I hated yesterday and wasn't looking forward to today. But I wanted to live. How selfish of me. I've been crying more than usual lately; I have survivor's guilt.

Like how dare I be upset about how things are going, and my aunt died. I'm nervous because I like writing my feelings out, but it's still painful. Keeping good spirits is so hard to do. There's been a day or two where I smiled and genuinely felt happy. I walked miles, I felt good, ate, and things seemed to pick up. I met someone in the midst of all this. I'm sure nothing will come out of it, but he sure kept me busy laughing, which helped through the most impossible days. He checked on me daily. I felt loved even if it was short-lived, I'll take it. Outside of my close friends and family. We went out to grab some breakfast, went to his place, talked and listened to music, but I knew that I would never see him again. He talked a good game, but of course, I knew those lines. Hell, I invented some them. God kept removing people from my life, but somehow as always, my old friend comes walking through the door. Year after year we go through the motions, but we're always connected. I don't know why, but it's something that remains. I'm always good in his presence, secured physically, but emotionally has always been a downfall. He somehow reminded me of my father. Finally, back at work and I still feel out of place. I knew I didn't belong here. I dreamed of turning in my two weeks' notice, but not yet. Yet, I'm here because every penny counts. These wires are killing me, but I'm handling it. Some days I feel like I'll be good; others I wonder how long it would take on the operating room table. I overdid it working too hard on my first day back. But I was glad to be a part of the world again. After a few hours, I started thinking about everything I've been through wondering if I invested enough time into myself. I shared my pain with my aunt physically, emotionally, and mentally. I knew I changed forever. I see the world in a different light. I'm ready to say it, fuck all this shit and live out my dreams, how much I owe. Everyone says they're glad I caught it early, but I knew God sat me down to figure this out. This journey had nothing to do with how I recovered from surgery. My vision gets clearer every moment but still blurry, I'm not ready to accept what I really want. A great friend told me to trust the process and embrace every emotion. When it hurts cry, when it's funny, laugh harder, and it's okay to feel weak. Don't let other people feelings dictate how you recover. Do the work and rest at your best.

June 22, 2019

Second day at work and feeling excited to see everyone, but somehow, I'm mentally done with this place. My workplace played a great deal in my life. When do I really live my life? I must go to another location, but I don't want to do that either. I'm grateful to have a job, but I know there's something else. I need to be doing something new at this point. God is changing me because things that used to upset me don't bother me at all. Oh well!

June 25, 2019

Up early for work. I have a doctor's appointment today. First time visiting my cardiologist since my surgery. Also, my first day at the new location in Rosslyn. I met some cool people. Just miss my old team. I respect things change, but I wasn't expecting this kind of change. Oh! I accidentally responded to Sean's message. Once I noticed I did it, there was no turning back Truthfully, I wasn't mad afterward. We've been talking consistently every day since. I finally told him I had open-heart surgery. He was shocked. Sometimes I wondered if that night never happened. Would I have gotten the support I was looking for in someone else? I guess you're wondering what night and what happened. Well, I used to work directly across the street from this beautiful hotel. When Sean and I used to date, we would get a room and spend time together. Things moved so fast. I couldn't tell if we were dating for a few months or years. Anyhow, it was the weekend and my per usual turn-up except I never wanted to be this drunk, but it happened. Sean wanted to get married and eventually isolate me from my family. He had his phone out and went live for the world to see him proposing to me. Thankfully, not many people were watching because he doesn't have many friends. I damn near fainted from the humiliation of him thinking he was even worthy of something like that. I literally just talked to his child's mother the other day and the things she told me made complete sense as to why he's the way he is now. I let him put the ring on because I was curious of what it would look like and what his type of style is. The ring literally scratched my finger from being so thin and cheap. Before I got the chance to let him down properly/nice, people were calling me and congratulating me on something I had no idea about at the time. He finally told me what he did, and I went off. I was so drunk I can't even remember half the words I said to him or did to him. We stayed up all night blaming each other about shit that made no sense to what just happened. I was just embarrassed because I was talking trash about him and how much of a deadbeat he was to his kids. He was lazy and always wanted to the easy way out. I woke up the next morning on the floor naked with a shot of Hennessey left beside me. Yes, immediately drunk it. I got the nerve to be judging someone. I just wondered if things would have been different. Of course not, that's why it didn't work out. Anyway, he asked if I wanted him to go to my doctor's appointments with me. I said yes because I hated going by myself and my low-key wanted to see him. I was so afraid of who I was now that I brought along Sean. He was something familiar from my past. I hated my past, but Sean was something to hang on to. He gave me another reason to procrastinate anything coming to into the future. He showed up on time. When he saw my scars, I saw his too. Mine was physical; his was in his eyes. I had another appointment my stress test. He was there for that too. I wasn't surprised he was by my side; I was surprised I didn't say anything sooner. It was something missing. I just didn't know what now. We had our differences but wasn't bad enough to hate him forever. Besides, I was given a second change. Maybe we can be friends. That's all my heart could take at this very moment. I wanted to feel safe and secured but something was telling me different. I saw the struggle in his weight loss. He needed something and he was broke. A part of my old habits showed up taking care of my temporary needs.

June 27, 2019

As time winds down, it's my last day here at my old workplace. I realized how much I'll miss my crew. I wondered if they would miss me as well. We had a great few years here. Another doctor appointment went well, but a lot changed and forever will change. I'm a cardiac patient. I stopped by to see some co-workers I worked with for some time. Pictures and memories will last forever.

July 4, 2019

It's been a while. Sometimes it's painful looking at this writing, but then again, it's my sanity. It was nice being around family, laughing and joking. Of course, the rain washed us out, but we still made the best of it. My aunt was missed. It was the first family event without her. We made it through. I enjoyed the kids. Watching them play it brought a calm to my soul. I've noticed all my cousins and family were romantically involved or married. Here I sat, broken and still.

July 5, 2019

I got to work, did as much as I could do, considering my credentials hasn't been working properly since the location change. Sean texted me that morning about a job interview he had. He got the job. We celebrated slightly. I was having a bad day. It's clear I wanted to hear those words, "What would make you happy?" But I knew he couldn't do that for me. I needed to make myself happy. I needed to get in a safe place for me. He wanted to be my hero, but I needed him to fall back and let me get through this. He *never* listened to me and what I need in this process. He wanted to be the reason I was better or okay, but the truth was I wasn't okay and needed more than he could provide.

July 6, 2019

Returned to work after being with my family. Saturdays are so boring here. It's already quiet during the week. The weekend is a struggle. It gives me time to look over my life. I must say I'm not where I want to be, but I'm nowhere near where I used to be. I've met some great people here. Even with the short time, they have challenged me in a new way. They treated me well and were very understanding about my situation. Two o'clock takes forever. You can do some much around here and time still moves slow. Oh well!

July 7, 2019

Praying things will get better with my health. I'm slowly pushing through. I spent my days filling out applications. My job location was closing here too soon enough. I asked my district manager twice about the rumors of closing. I got the company policy answer after seven years of service—yes and no. Confusing, right? I understand, but I also understand that it's time to leave and make moves for myself. I put in about twenty-five applications. Out of all of them, one stood out the most to me: the *mission*. I read the qualifications at least ten times, thinking I would do great here. I put in my resume, crossed my fingers, and left things as is. After a couple more, I finally decided to give myself a break. Watch a little TV and write. Writing and still thinking about the *mission*. I started thinking how I might qualify and what if I really got the job. Another day I prayed for better. In Jesus' name I pray.

July 16, 2019

I woke up feeling the good energy today. Work wasn't too bad either. I had a doctor's appointment. Of course, Sean was going to be there with me. I must say he hasn't missed an appointment yet, but I was skeptical of his presence. After my doctor's appointment and feeling a little down because some things were getting better and others needed work, we decided to go to the museum. We had a great time together. We barely looked at the exhibits. I've been talking his head off about this job at the *mission*, and in the mist of enjoying each other, I got that email I was looking for about an interview. I was excited and nervous because I didn't know was it would say. Now, my new conversation was how nervous I am until I go on the interview.

July 19, 2019

OMG! Today is finally here. I'm so freaking nervous and excited. This interview means a lot to me. I ordered a ride because I didn't want to be late, and the ride helps calm my nerves. I felt good going to the place. As my driver pulled up, I thought to myself, *WTF am I doing? I can't handle this panel interview. A few people asking questions about my skills and experiences. I hope I can keep it together.* After the first ten minutes, my nerves started to relax. I felt comfortable but stayed alert. This one lady walked me around to see the place, and I was so dizzy and nauseous. My legs wanted to give in, but I kept moving. I felt good about this interview. I left feeling good and wondering if I could possibly sit at that table one day telling my story. I did more research and found that I might be more connected than I thought. This career path may be exactly what I need. As I was riding home picturing myself in the role, my mom asked if I wanted to go to the casino. Of course I jumped on the opportunity, because it was more than gambling, which I like. I got the chance to kick it with moms outside of the house and hospital. Slots and the crab cakes were the bomb too.

July 20–24, 2019

I've had four okay days. Of course I've had my lightheadedness, dizziness, and feeling like I'm crazy. I've been telling people and my doctors that I don't feel right. Everyone tells me that they think I went back to work too soon, but I know in my body that something wasn't right. Most importantly, I knew I had to go back. I was dying on the inside mentally, emotionally, and spiritually. I've never been this weak or insecure in my life. Feeling weird through my whole body with no explanation is confusing, frustrating, annoying, and makes me moody. Sometimes walking is a huge challenge for me. I pray every day that I get better or at least stay focus on the victory at the end. Crying is like my first cousin—we go everywhere together. Most time, I don't even talk about what I go through because I figure people get tired of hearing what's going on with me. Through all the hard times, I'm still finding a way to smile. I love the fact that I still try my hardest to fight through whatever comes my way with the help of *God*.

July 25–27, 2019

Woke up feeling okay. I got plans to go to my school to register for classes. My mother came along with me, my true ride-or-die. She'd been holding me down since day one. After registering, I suddenly started feeling lightheaded, but I thought I could shake it off and not say anything. She wanted to go to Union Station, which I was cool with doing. Unfortunately, my body started to feel shaky, nauseous, hot, and super fatigue, and my entire body was sore. I thought that if sat down and got myself together, I would be okay, but I ended up in the hospital again. I've been trying to figure out what's been going on with my body. I thought that my heart was fixed and healed. I've been going through a series of tests. These doctors are awesome, but the waiting game is so hard, especially when you go on the internet to diagnose yourself. Shit! I should have been dead. Well, I'll be in the hospital overnight until they can do some more tests tomorrow. Every time I think that I'm on my way to being better, I'm pushed back or sat down. At first I kept thinking about all the things that I had to do. Then I thought about how I lost my relationship with God. I started getting comfortable without praying and praising him. After those tests were done, they needed to do another one. Finally, they did a tilt table test, and I was officially diagnosed with postural orthostatic tachycardia syndrome (POTS). I have no idea what that is yet. I've never even heard of it. It has no cure, but sometimes it can be manageable if you follow the diet. Medicine can be used if needed, but there are chances that it can get worse. Here I was thinking, *Oh Lord, why me again? Yet I never thought about thanking you for another day on this earth to get it right.* I have Sean here with me. He drives me crazy, but it's good to have company. He was asking questions as if he was my husband. I knew what he was doing, trying to impress me as if I gave two shits about him pretending to care about what's really going on with my health. He knew that if he showed up, he would eat. Hey, I'm not mad at the hustle. I think he stole twenty dollars out of my wallet. SMDH. I don't think I know; I know that he's a bum for real. I just wanted company and he was available. I asked him about it; he still lied, but I knew. Desperation at a new level. Saturday evening is here, and I have orders to follow and home tomorrow.

July 28, 2019

My third day here. My stomach was very tight, and I feel nauseous with a headache. Still feeling uncomfortable here. I had an unsettling feeling in my soul. I didn't know what it was, but I knew that it wasn't a good thing. My mom came to see me, which always brightens my day. My son called me. I was happy to see his face on Facetime, but his voice wasn't assuring at all. He told me that he was on his way home, but I knew that his eyes were lying to me. After a few hours, I knew that that unsettling feeling was my son being missing. Even in the hospital, we called everywhere looking for him. Oddly enough, a police officer doing rounds on my floor comes in just to check on patients, asking if we were okay after a small incident in the hospital. I asked about my son because he could clearly see that something was wrong with me besides an illness. He thinks he heard something about my son's name on his radio. He made a few phone calls, and within ten minutes, a guy called about my son. Surely, any mother dreads this call from an unknown source asking, "Are you the mother of this child?" The guy, however, did tell me that he had my son. Unfortunately, for all the wrong reasons: robbery. Bewildered and puzzled as to why he would do that was an understatement to the relief that I felt knowing that he wasn't *dead*. Pissed but grateful that he was okay. Now on top of my situation with my health, my stress levels increased. Ashamed and embarrassed, I slowly called my uncle, who was always there for me no matter what or the time. He didn't ask any questions; he just agreed to help me out. Honestly, I was happy that he didn't, because if I had to answer any questions, I would have broken down literally into pieces. The rest of the night was a blur.

July 29, 2019

The next day, I was released from the hospital. I was still trying to hold it together as I wasn't at my best. It was midafternoon. Riding with my uncle to get my son's belongings was humiliating as hell. Here I was doing all I can to redeem myself for the mother I once was. Look at me now getting all my bullshit back. The pain and torture I gave out, I'm finally receiving it now. At least that's what it felt like. The nerve of me thinking that this surgery and the outcome would change my past overnight. I figured that with this happening, I would change and everything else would follow. All mistakes would vanish. Hopefully, this will be a lesson learned for us. Let the day takes its course. OMG! More work to do. I must register for classes before it's too late. In the midst of it all, I'm trying to get my documents together for my new job, which I look forward to starting. I need a fresh start in the real world.

July 30, 2019

I took a couple of days to relax and energize myself. I need to get my spirit back together before starting my new job. Got a doctor's appointment with my primary care doctor after my hospital stay again. She's pretty good. She ordered the same thing: high salt and water diet. I followed the doctor's orders, but my body knew that I needed more. I'm finally on the water/salt pills, which help keep the water and salt in my vessels instead of me trying to do it alone. Sean was with me for entertainment purposes. My appointments are never boring because I have company. It was fun, at least, and my wallet was close to me this time around.

August 1, 2019

Woke up ready to go to the doctors, only because I had another bad day. Now, here she ordered that I double up on my pills, and increase water and salt more often than usual. I finally accepted the fact that I must slow down and take things one day, sometimes one moment, at a time. It's very frustrating living with POTS. Sometimes it feels as if you're crazy, like it's all in your head. The good thing about that part is it's not all in your head; it's a real thing. And you're not alone. Others have this illness too. Praying that this gets better. Every day I wake up, I have a chance for a new testimony.

August 4, 2019

Woke up, took my meds, and went to church. On our way, we always listen to a preacher on the radio. It's like getting a double dose of church, which I needed ever so badly. I've been persistently going to church. I wasn't sure if I was going to satisfy my own soul or I wanted to be close to my uncle. Either way, I felt momentarily comfortable, but I knew that I have work to do with redeeming my soul and being forgiven. As bad as I wanted to be whole again, I couldn't shake the hatred that I had burning inside of me that God took my aunt away and I had to be sober. Service was uplifting, and later that afternoon, my uncle gave me some bone fish that were very delicious. I cooked them myself and it was my first time. I can cook, but I just hate it. I'd rather wash dishes. Went through some pictures reminiscing through old times. All my days weren't always about working, playing men, and partying. Except I can't deny that Four Seasons stays and riding in foreign cars were a luxury most people will never experience. My dirt was always done solo, but I was confronted by my aunt when she saw something that transpired. I can still hear her voice: "You know it comes with a price." My girlfriends and I at the time enjoyed learning more about our culture and exploring history that was beyond us. Sometimes I wondered how I missed my blessings every day. Oh! Never mind alcohol, and getting money was a priority.

August 5, 2019

Still at my old job, thankful for having a job. My Rosslyn team has been good to me through my illness; they have really treated me well. Looking for a new job is exhausting but well worth the trouble. I'm keeping my fingers crossed and prayed up. Through all these things, Sean has been helping me get through the hard parts. I didn't like traveling alone as it triggered my anxiety. But I knew that he was always around for something. Money was always a factor when he was around, and I didn't mind helping. I felt like at least I can feed him. Poor thing be so hungry all the time. His weight is down again, and I've noticed how his eyes are sunk in. I'm just thankful for the surface support, at the least. My family has played a huge part in my healing, especially my mother.

August 6, 2019

It's raining and it sounds good against my windowpane. So I opened the window—it was the best feeling in the world. I looked through some meals to make for this special diet I must be on from the doctor's orders. I've seen a few I really liked and looked delicious too. Oh well! Let me just relax and listen to the rain. This kind of peace doesn't come often.

August 8, 2019

Up at it again. On my way to my doctor's appointment. Sean is meeting me there. I was looking at him and that was another day that I noticed that he lost a lot weight. Also, I was happy that he was there because everyone knows that I hate being in the street alone with POTS. It's the craziest shit ever! I found myself crying more than ever today. I couldn't hold any tears back. I went home looking for a therapist because I needed someone other than my family to say that I was normal or it's life and things would eventually change. I've gotten on my knees every day, praying things would change or get better. I pray for God to remove Sean out of my life without so many words and I prayed for myself. I know that this will be a *toxicship*. Prayer changes everything.

August 9, 2019

Woke up feeling okay. Showered, ate breakfast, and took my meds. Waiting on my uncle to take me to the station to go to work. Made it there safe. OMG! Back to feeling nauseous and lightheaded. Mercy, just breathe through it. Okay, I got through that moment. Thank you, God! I need to exercise to get my blood circulating the correct way. I did a twenty-minute workout on the recumbent bike. My legs were a little tired, but I felt a little better. Left work feeling a little more confident than I was before. I go through a lot more than what

I tell people. I'm at the point where saying "I'm fine" is a habit. I don't want to talk about it. I listen to everyone that I find myself trying to fix their problems. Oh! I forgot to tell my story.

August 10, 2019

Another day in church with my uncle. Jesus brings the word every Sunday. My faith falls, but I try. God brings me to my feet. Back home and Sean's here. I missed him, but I don't love this man. I sometimes struggle to do anything with this. We're always at each other's throats, mainly because I don't want a relationship. I just wanted a friend through the hard parts, but apparently it doesn't work like that. Breakfast was good. We talked, and that's when I realized that he was just familiar from my past. I didn't want a relationship with him.

August 13, 2019

Listening in on this Monday call, looking around as I hear and see people putting in their resignation letters. Feeling annoyed but honestly jealous because I'm still feeling stuck here. Well, since I'm here, might as well get some things done. Through all this, I'm still checking on the status on the new position at the new job. I need to find some light exercises for my POTS and build a little strength again. My boss asked me to create a job opening. People just don't want to travel the distance for little money and it's part-time. When you wait on the Lord, things are always worth it and right. As I huff and puff about still being the last one standing, I got the call. I was offered the position at the *mission*. Looking through clothes always makes me happy. Fashion always does it for me. Ordering books for classes as well. Getting a head start. I keep looking at my account. Something doesn't look right, but maybe things will change itself. It's always hard reading these accounts especially since the new changes.

I look at cars thinking what it would be like to drive. Silly dream, because I'm still not cleared or I don't have the right to do so.

August 27, 2019

Woke up ready, yet nervous. I feel confident and optimistic. Got a nice welcome to my new job. They had everything ready for me. I brought my lunch, but I was treated to lunch there. My next few hours at work were so difficult because my POTS wasn't doing so good, but I pushed through. I grabbed on the walls, barely walking a straight line. I just knew that someone would figure me out and I would be a liability to my job, but I got off early that first day, thank God.

August 30, 2019

Today, my son is an official high schooler. I can't believe that he's in the ninth grade. Where did the time go? On another note, I looked exactly how I feel—horrible. I look like I'm in an abusive relationship with POTS. I honestly need ten hours of sleep, which doesn't always help because after all that sleep or rest, I'm still fatigued. After three days of work, I'm praying that I don't need to be in the hospital again. Sickness! Never give up, but school stresses me out too. Now I'm here thinking about what my topic will be for my paper. Barely getting it together without passing out or throwing up on everyone who passes me. Ugh, today is so brutal, but I must play it cool. Also, Sean started working at my old job. I didn't mind because I was leaving anyway. He lost his job as a security guard. Well, the contract ended, according to what he said. He worked front desk, which didn't make much, but it put money in the pocket for the meantime, especially with two kids and child support hitting hard. I've always tried to be professional at work, but somehow he always wanted me to show him that he's my man even though it was *clear* that there's no romantic relationship and he was not my man. I'm completely done with him, but I hated seeing people down. I know what rock-bottom feels like.

August 31, 2019

Good morning. Damn, it's so difficult to get out of bed. My body hurts so bad. Whenever I told someone, I usually got the same response: You're probably overdoing it lately. But what they didn't know is even if I did nothing, my body would find a way to become off balance. I'm no longer interested in expressing how I feel or how these mood swings change daily, yet I mastered a smiling face. At my job, it's the third day and nothing on my body is working right. I can't even type. My body is not signaling with my brain. I want to run in the bathroom and cry, but I can't. My face shows struggle, but I must push further, right? People only know what I tell them or what they assume. I can't give off too much because I don't know these people. Moreover, I still haven't found a topic for my paper for school. I have a few ideas, but I'm just not sure which direction I want to go. I usually go home and watch other people's biographies or listen to their own story. The one factor that never changed in anyone's story is believing in themselves. Except I have someone depending on me 24/7. There's no room for "drop everything and figure out life" or "shoot for the stars." I guess I planned backward, but there's still time for something better.

September 3, 2019

Washed my hair, feeling a little better today. Low-key feeling some type of way because my hair is thinning. I know how it happened, but I was desperate to get my hair done. I wanted to believe that it was my fault, not taking care of my hair like I should. Well, most days I barely lifted my arms without needing a break or nap. I slowly curled my hair and wrapped it, but it turned out that I'll be wearing a ponytail for the day. I was looking at some clothes online. I love clothes. The thought of how people transform when they put on something nice. I don't value the money; I value the art in it. Found myself at work taking pictures and trying to find myself between this plastered smile and tears.

September 4, 2019

Today is the new staff orientation at the DC location. I'm happy because it's closer to me. Also, I enjoyed the training and the speakers were cool. This place has a lot of history, and I'm happy to be a part of something bigger than myself. After hearing about some ways to eat better and healthy, I've been looking up all kinds of food. I even got the chance to do some retail shopping at the boutiques near my old job. Still miss working there, not the job but the environment and the people I personally worked alongside with in DC.

September 5, 2019

Up early, felt okay, showered, ate, and took my medicine. I will say I believe I smiled more today than I have in a long time. I'm at work training on how things work at my new job. The organization seems great. It's something to be a part of, for sure. Some of the people are questionable, but that's at every job and a part of life with people.

September 6, 2019

Today is payday, and I'm confused about how they pay us if we don't have direct deposit yet. I get there at about 9:30 a.m. Around 10 o'clock, this lady comes in the building holding the checks—yes, paper checks. I can't even remember when I was paid with a paper check. Nevertheless, she seemed cool, had a nice smile, and was very helpful. Also, it was like she was building a team for something later and she needed soldiers. I was in need to deposit my check, but I had to wait because I didn't have ID. I left my wallet in my other purse. Friday was very awkward and fast. I was happy when the day was over. I was sick and tired.

September 17, 2019

OMG! I'm used to working on Saturday, but things picked up so fast. I wasn't ready, but it gave me purpose. I truly met some amazing people this weekend. We even have the same mission to do similar things in life. I adore people like that. Saturdays are super busy here, but I enjoy fast-paced days. We were all talking about stories of where we came from. I tried to keep my personal life out of it as much as I could, but my truth released everything I had inside me. Great for me that these people have a heart of gold. They treated me with respect and checked on me in ways that melts my heart, except I felt horrible with my health. I kept trying to force happiness upon my face, but my emotions and illness wouldn't let me do that.

September 18, 2019

After a bad day yesterday, I tried to push through swollen eyes and a broken spirit. I continued to do so because deep down inside I was happy to be alive. I just couldn't find a way to get through this heavy guilt, frustration, anger, and pain. All the people at the job are strangers, so I can't confide in them. Walked around aimlessly, hoping to find a little part of me again that made sense. God sat within me, so all those other thoughts are not possible at all.

September 22, 2019

The day I decided to cut my hair. It was falling out anyway. I was excited to do something different with my hair. I enjoyed the look, but I knew that winter was around the corner. I got plenty of compliments, and the freedom was good, of not having hair on my neck. The streaks gave me some life with it. I went to the bank to put some money in my account. I have this illusion that one day I'll be able to move, but this sickness really scares me sometimes. I'm not sure I can make it on my own being sick. Some days I think I have it under control. The next day it's like a nightmare and I can't wake up. I'm trying to come to terms that I might need someone around me forever. Not to solely take care of me, but make sure that things are okay with me. I'm not okay with that, but that's my new reality. My sister came to see me. I love being around my sister/cousin. She's so damn funny, I can be around her any day until we have too much of each other, then we start fighting. LOL.

September 24, 2019

Back at work and I'm still learning the ropes. Things are pretty good for the most part. Some people are very genuine and others like to get over. I was taking pictures in the bathroom when I noticed that my face has gotten a little fat. I look pregnant, but I know that I'm not. I gained thirty-seven pounds easily. Eating and no exercise. I've enjoyed eating any and everything with no regrets. Now, I must put a diet together. I'm probably not going to follow through with this, but I want to, though. It's almost been a month here. I don't miss my old job at all. I do miss the people. Seven years are difficult to just walk away from and act like you don't know people anymore. Honestly, it was a hard loss for me too. Being around the same people for seven years, it was like a relationship too. You'll fight, make up, and do it all over again.

September 25, 2019

Finally, I decided to investigate some insurance benefits. The HR lady is super cool. Very professional and approachable. Not to mention she looks like me in one of those positions you don't rarely see. My day consists of a lot of water and salt. I was introduced to this young lady named Angie. She was easy to read. She was stern but soft at the same time. We instantly clicked. She lived close to my house on the other side of Maryland. She offered me a ride home. I quickly declined, not because I didn't want the ride. I was used to struggling through. I didn't realize that someone was just being nice. The day was winding down, and before she left, she offered one more time. I changed my mind, ultimately because I wasn't feeling well and the Metro was going to be a challenge to get home. I would have never thought that a simple ride home would turn into a true bond. We talked about our background, which was mostly similar except that she was more South than me. I told her about my surgery and POTS. She never heard of POTS, but she sure seemed genuine to know about it. Arriving home, we agreed to ride to work together. Let's just say the rest was history. Friends forever!

September 26, 2019

Today is exciting, not for me, but for a very special co-worker. She has an amazing anniversary celebration today. She put in more than forty years at this place. Prepping and making sure that she didn't know what's happening was hard. Most people think that they must talk to her differently, but trust me, she hipped to everything. Even the small things we never think about. Anyway, I watched people flow back and forth. As they all saluted Mary on her well-deserved celebration, one lady stood out because she said that she and Mary were good friends. Her children loved Mary as she had known her for forty years. I noticed how she looked frantically for her notes to talk about Mary. It seemed so cliché that for a person you've known for forty years, you need a piece of paper or a sticky note to remember your friendship. It wasn't even good stories. Just typically surface bullshit people say at parties to make themselves feel good that they mention something. Angie and I adore Mary. She's a straight shooter, yet so gentle. We took pictures together, three good faces. As time dwelled down, it was time for the grand finale. Her nephew came in the door and Mary lost it, in a good way. Her expression was priceless, not for us but for the love she has for him. She listened to everyone tell their version of their relationship or bond with Mary. All I can say is she was sweet to me from the beginning. I needed the microphone to confirm what we built. She always kept it real. She's familiar with her ways. She reminds me of my aunt.

September 28, 2019

Finally off work and now I'm on my way to Rosslyn to meet a friend. I love going out to Rosslyn. It was always peaceful, and the people were friendly. They have one of the best nail shops around the DMV. The condos and apartments are always breathtaking. The communities and accessibilities were on point. We would walk for hours just talking and making plans. It seemed genuine for the moment. I never felt completely sure about things. It was mostly an eggshell relationship—one wrong move and everything cracks open. More so abusive. I know sometimes we like to assume. When we first hear abusive, we instantly think about physical wounds. I, too, assume. I assumed because we weren't in a relationship, just friends. Our friendship was tested by how much pain I could endure. I started living in the moment, because anything beyond that was too much to handle. What a waste! Maybe I'll feel better in the morning.

September 29, 2019

I woke up feeling a little off-balance. I ignored it as much as I could before things started to change out of my control. I started feeling nauseous, dizzy, and extremely fatigued. I was on my way to fainting. It was just a matter of time when. We went to a bagel shop. I love an everything bagel, but while waiting for it to be done, my health was suddenly changing. I started having clampy hands and sweats, even though it's a bit chilly outside. After visually noticing my symptoms, I caught a straight ride home. That was the longest ride of my life. Not the distances, but the struggle to keep the food down. I finally got home and got out of the car, only to realize that my legs wouldn't move as they should. They felt like jelly, and the ground was like soft clouds with no stability. My entire body was weak and shaky. I needed a break every two steps with the help of my son. I could foresee the future of going to the emergency room. Once I got in the house, I quickly lay down. It was short-lived. My anxiety started flaring up. Everything was now an issue. My son asked me a thousand times if I want to go to the emergency room. I answered no, but my body answered *yes*! Finally going to the hospital; to get to the back was quick. Waiting patiently to see the doctors was the hard game. My son was sitting with me and never once seemed bothered. I loved the fact that he wanted to be next to me during my rough times. Yet I felt weak because I've always been there for him. Once again, there was nothing to be done. Just a bunch of apologies about not having enough information to make things better or a cure. After getting home, all I did was cry endlessly, but when someone texts me, I tell them that I was going or coming from the hospital. Most people got so used to it that they stop asking me what happened. I started researching about POTS myself. I always Googled the symptoms but never investigated it as if others weren't suffering or dealing with the same thing. I just happened to look on the internet and had seen so many #POTS post. I read so many posts of people just like me dealing with the different symptoms each day. The crazy part about POTS is the majority of your symptoms are never the same. They tell you to write down your symptoms to see if there's a pattern or maybe you'll know your own trigger points. Nope, every day is a different day with something you can't explain. Truthfully, you don't even want to. I prayed constantly, asking God to take this away from me. Then I started thanking him: "Even with this, you still allow me to get through." It's difficult, but I'm no stranger to pushing through a dark place or time.

October 4, 2019

Woke up and got ready for another doctor's appointment. At this point, I felt hopeless. I'm just going because they said to follow up with a neurologist as well as my cardiologist. They knew that it wasn't anything with my heart, that that was fine. They figured, "Maybe we should send you to a neurologist. Something could be related to the brain." After doing several tests, he concluded that it wasn't anything with my coordination. He did the stand-up and sit-down test to check my blood levels. Now, he said he didn't see any big changes in my levels going up or down, but most times when I feel the worst, I'm alone. By the time I make it to the doctor, I might be having a good day, but that doesn't mean that I am getting better. It's just a good day, there's a difference. I'll take it. The doctor also checked my weight. I've gained a bit more all in the right places for me anyway. I must say, my neurologist seemed too busy to care for patients that had insurance through the government. I might be supersensitive because things are different than what I thought. At this time, I thought I would be farther along with my health and certain situations. Besides, my cardiologist said that a little weight won't hurt to help my wires from hurting me. The results of this visit included giving me some pills to help with the dizziness. Hopefully, this helps along with all the other medicines I'm taking. What do you take for a broken spirit? People often tell me that I look tired. I'm just at my lowest. Have you ever seen life at the level of ant?

October 31, 2019

It's Halloween, and I'm glad this month is almost over. My sister didn't get to celebrate her birthday with us. Her dad was in the hospital. My uncle had a stroke and a heart attack. *I hate this fucking year!* Working lightened the hatred I had. My co-workers were in spirit, but all I wanted was the month to be over. Every second felt like an hour.

November 16, 2019

Riding to work, I decided to reach out to an old friend. I texted him knowing I'll get a response, of course. I didn't know what it would be; I didn't care if it was negative or positive. I just knew that he would respond. I asked him if he missed me. He replied that he used to when I was around. Damn, he missed me. That was shocking news, but cool. Shit, I thought he didn't have feelings. Opinions, yes, but feelings left me puzzled considering. He lived through street codes and protocols with an honest job. After trying to think of what to say next, I waited because I wasn't sure what I really wanted from him. Okay, that's a lie, I knew exactly what I wanted. It has never been about sex. However, side-eye action to my girlfriends, I've craved and endlessly chase that person he showed me once. Shortly after, I got a text saying he's been trying to connect to tell me in person that he got a daughter that just turned one. He wanted me to hear it from him first. My entire body melted and hit the floor. I read it a million times hoping that I read it wrong or could change the story. We've been on and off for seven years. Every time we were off, it was always a new surprise for me. I was so choked up behind this because we talked about me having a daughter before, and promises were made. I was crushed that another woman took my promise without warning, even though I knew in my gut that he wasn't a good man for me. I just needed to feed those insecurities, and when they weren't fulfilled, I could blame him for it. Fuck it! I didn't want to live through the burn and I want him to give me more of what I didn't have—a filled heart. I've been yearning to fill this hole in my heart. He couldn't do what Daddy should have—love me the proper way. I was raised to be strong, and a leader is never vulnerable. Sister girls live through the burn; it's not worth the bandage that will be ripped off again and again. I know that I'll never have him the way I want and need, so I sent my blessings from a far. OMG! How I love that man. I guess it wasn't all his fault. Hell, I ducked so many calls and bullshitted. I felt like I was teaching him a lesson about missing me, only to realize that I was teaching him how to live without me. I kept thinking to myself, *If I were around, would that have been me with child?* Living the conversations we talked about in the future. He sent a text asking if I was busy. Of course! I wanted to see him, but I was busy running away from more exhausting news. New York was just what I needed. Besides, I knew that he wanted to apologize through sex. Now, I know what you're thinking. He just wants sex, but that was our love language. We can hold a conversation easily, but our way of doing things were through lovemaking. We showed our love, pain, and disappointments through sex. When we were done, there were no words to be spoken. He would gently, yet firmly, bite and kiss my butt cheek. We would shower, and I would lie on his chest until morning, where I was greeted with a forehead kiss, which I adored because I've always been ashamed of my forehead when I younger. Damn! A baby.

November 28, 2019

Time has gotten away from me. I really didn't care. Everything's been falling apart anyway. It's Thanksgiving and I'm the most ungrateful person walking this earth today. Everything feels like a loss. I was volunteering at my job. We prepared everything we needed to start working. As time moved, so did my attitude. I enjoyed doing this for the children, the best thing yet. I told myself that I didn't want to be here, only because I was afraid of what was new to me. God knows I miss my aunt and I'm still shattered. I'm going to always feel incomplete without her. I know we're not supposed to get it, but I'm still baffled. We never knew that we would lose Cindy, especially the way it happened. My co-workers made the day easier and fun. I learned the true definition of commitment. I wanted no parts of this day or event at first. I got home and looked around, noticing that I still have people around me who love me and being grateful that I'm alive.

December 6, 2019

We are celebrating my best friend's/sister's birthday today. Damn, we've really been hanging in there. I guess it's safe to say that I don't have commitment issues. Twenty years of friendship. We all went out to dinner. We ate and caught up with each other. We've all been through a rough year. Spending time with them really helped me get back and focus, not that I fell off but writing my thoughts out on paper. We chilled in my parking lot an extra two hours reminiscing about all the shit we did and what we've been through. The secrets we hold are worthy of a show. I couldn't imagine being with any other people but them.

December 8, 2019

Today wasn't a good day. I was so mentally, physically, and spiritually tired, but seeing my uncle always makes life better. Most of my days are spent trying not to fall out or staying calm to avoid an anxiety attack. We spent hours up there with him. I was hurt that couldn't get to him as I want or should. I know that he understands because he knows my condition as well. Kyree was there too, which also made me happy. My uncle loves that boy. I hope Kyree really makes him proud one day, especially with all the trouble we went through when he got locked up twice. After coming home feeling a little down, I started looking at clothes—it's my happy place. I felt down because I'm always stuck in the middle of guilty or tired.

December 25, 2019

Today is the day that I decided to stop writing, not because I don't want to anymore. I think I'm going to let God and nature take its course. I've battled addiction, depression, toxic relationships, myself, and death. Besides, I wonder where I will be next year with my health, mentally, physically, and spiritually. Who knows? I'll spend my new time making better choices and living as much as I can. I don't know what God and POTS have in store for me, but I'm hoping great things and a brighter future. As bad as this year has been, maybe I'll finish this year with a bit of hope. Thank you for letting me share my deepest thoughts with you. Leaving this here might bring some unsettled clarity.

April 24, 2020

Well, it is me again! I was looking forward to telling you some awesome news or some shit that would blow your mind and go down in history. It was urgent that I pick this pen up versus a bottle. I just knew that this year would be refreshing, but damn! I wanted a lot of bullshit and people out of my life for good. So I told Sean that I was pregnant and borrowed some lady's sonogram off the internet, and sent it to him just so he would leave me alone. I had this burning desire to see if things were missing with me and my old friend. I clearly explained to him that I wanted to talk. He obliged and, silly me, I thought we would really talk. We fucked, and every stroke felt like goodbye or that's how I felt, because I knew that that was my goodbye gift to him. I will miss it. LOL. He looked deep in my eyes, but I could not see anything other than the surface. Let's just say that it was another closed chapter. Okay, partially closed when it comes to him. We all have that one toxic drink worth the fix. Even if it's temporary, it works. I loved it all about him—the hurting feelings, the happy times, the smiles, the sex, the friendship, the unspoken pieces, and I loved him. I started evaluating myself. I will admit that I played a part in these hurt feelings. Expectations will damage you if you put them on other people, because you're the only one left with the results. Oh! Not every man hurt me; I was toxic to some men too. I brought in a lot of baggage I did not notice I was carrying. I was just always fucking tired. Most baggage I had nothing to do with. It was just generational bullshit passed down and I picked it up like it was worthy treasures. I dropped loads on men who had no idea what to do with it. My background consists of two types: *love* and *survival*. I say that because I had plenty of love from so many people that half the time I did not recognize it because I was focused on surviving. It was at very young age where my survival instinct kicked in. I have never given myself the chance to love because I was still surviving in adulthood. I will honestly give myself a true chance moving forward. I am worthy of someone seeing me for who I am. I best believe that I am worthy of it all; you know I am, *babe*! I see you listening and have patience, whoever you are.

On another note, *2020* has completely showed its natural ass! Our president said that this virus was nothing to worry about. Yet the world is upside down. March 16 really gave us the go that something was truly *wrong*! Everything in Maryland was shut down by 5 p.m., all due to COVID-19. That was the last day I worked inside the building. It was weird because we were all just watching TV in the front lobby with no mask on. A lot of our part-time people lost their jobs, so quickly nobody really understood the seriousness this virus had on us. Many people were falling ill and dying from this virus.

April 25, 2020

Today is the day! I have officially made it through without a drink (alcoholic beverage) or a cigarette. Thanks to the good Lord and my determination to be *great*. I promised myself to never feel that low again. It was hard, but I did it. I did not celebrate out loud because I wanted to feel that kind of joy alone, the same way I felt that pain alone. This has shown me that this journey had nothing to do with heart surgery. It is all about the recovery transformation. I had every excuse to drink, and I am sure that no one would blame me, but I had one reason not to drink (*living*).

April 26, 2020

The days and hours have been passing me by. I have been wondering how my mom's in the hospital this time around. I have not been reaching out much. I talk to her, but honestly not as much as I should. I am truthfully terrified. I have watched my mom be strong for so many years and now I see tears in her eyes that was not from someone else's injury. Things may be different this time around, and I am not ready for any of this. I thought we got through the worst times, but I knew something was lurking around the corner. Shit was too quiet, and they said it is the calm before the storm; it really showed up. I pray for our world. God, please forgive us all.

May 2, 2020

I have gotten no sleep. My mom will not let me out of her sight. She has been going downhill. I'm afraid, I'm very afraid. She completely checked out and there is nothing I can do for her. I endlessly watched her health go down and come up. Where is my peace in all this? My family and close friends. Thank God I'm not drinking. Shit would surely be crazy. I reached out to an old friend's aunt, as he happened to have the same surgery as mine. It's crazy how God handles things when you let him work. Not to gloat in anyone's pain, but God will handle you appropriately. She said he's doing great and should be out of ICU soon. Then he called and told me. I was happy that God was showing him how I felt, except this round he will be alone. We talked every day leading up to the surgery. I honestly felt like my job is done with him. I needed to step back and let him recover on his own. I kept feeling guilty that if I left, I would be punished, but there was no love for me when it was my turn. I hated the fact that he never realized how lonely it feels in here. But I knew that he knew that the fear and anger shown toward the nurses showed his truth. He was afraid. My mom has scared the living shit out of me. The woman who I've known all my life by the name of superwoman fell short. It's known that we're all humans, but I didn't see this coming at all. Nearly a year ago, she was helping me prepare for my surgery. I feel like I can't give her what she gave me. I've been by her side the entire time. I went to my special friend's house because COVID-19 was about to make me insane. I had to find my own sanity and my son. I don't have any regrets because I truly needed the moment to regroup, even though someone close believed that if I didn't go, she would have never ended the way she did. It broke my heart that they would think like that. It was my way of dealing with it. My mom had been back and forth in the hospital, and things just won't get better for her.

May 3, 2020

Today was hell. No sleep at all again. My mom is slowly drifting away. I watched endlessly as she leaves here and comes back. She kept saying that she was holding on, but I wonder what's keeping her. For the first time in my life, I'm prepared to deal with the worst. I'm praying for the better, but today has confirmed that nothing is promised. My mom is my entire best friend in the world. She holds all my secrets as I hold hers. She holds my strength and I hold hers. Yes, she drives me crazy, LOL, but I love and would do anything for that woman. I need her to fight! Lord. Maybe I need to fight with and for her. I don't want to arrange my heart for death. I know it comes for everyone, but Lord, please not around my aunt's death anniversary. Mother's Day and Kyree's birthday are at the end the month. Today, my mom couldn't pull it together, so we had to call the ambulance to get her the help she needed. After hours of thinking, she was getting what she needed. She called historical as she left. She's not comfortable nowhere. It's 5:33 a.m. and she's still not happy or settled. I read her a Scripture out of the Bible that she always read me. I'm not sure if I made it worst or better for her, but at least I tried with the Lord.

May 4, 2020

The birds are officially chirping and I'm up as if sleeping came and gone. Fuck it! Another sleepless day.

May 6, 2020

Today was a great day thus far. Kyree got great news on his Zoom call. I guess what I've been saying finally kicked in. My old friend called me; I didn't answer. I honestly don't know why I was irritated or over the fact of entertaining him after what he did to me. I felt like the bigger person by talking to him before the surgery and even after, but I'm done pacifying the fact that he wasn't there for me and I should be there for him. He had the audacity to think that there would be more with us. I thought that it was clear that we're better as friends. That was what he chose to be, and I obliged. I missed the guy I met before. I missed the old him. We had such a connection, something different from sex and bullshit. I'm sorry I didn't miss him; I wanted the guy who put on his best behavior. Grant that we all do, but this guy was a complete devil in disguise. We all have a dark side where we get angry or upset, but this guy was deepening his anger and was better at hurting people. He knew that he was mean and crude, but he blamed me for *making* him this way. Interesting, right?

May 7, 2020

Today was just so hard. I just did not feel like doing anything. Not in that depressed way, but I just wanted to lie around and enjoy myself with no cares of anything. My old friend called me again, and I did not receive the call. Not that I missed it, but I just didn't answer. I'm struggling with resentment and guilt. A part of me is struggling because I resent him for not being there for me when I went through the same surgery. I mean, he truly left me high and dry. The other side of me feels guilty because I know how it feels to go through something like that and feel alone. We talk sometimes, but I hate it when he says things as if we are getting closer. We made it clear that the friendship was better than the relationship, which was not true. He knew that he was wrong and now he is feeling it more than ever. I almost do not want the friendship. Okay, I don't, but I feel like God would punish me for not wanting to listen to him. His voice annoyed me heavily. I hated everything he said and every move he made. I am done allowing men to walk over me and I remain loyal to what they thought was okay and crushing to me. I know who I am. I am a woman who knows she is better than this and much more worthy; my latest situation has proven this. Last year, I got a weak-ass "Happy Mother's Day" text from him. This year is a different approach with a different guy, someone I might want to date, and I feel it. We talk all about it—everything. He most definitely knows how to treat me and showed me what *love* feels like, especially because I now have it for myself. He is so dope! Understanding that love is not one way, but surely true, honest, and adorable. Love is my adorable language. Listen, laugh, and relate. Good nights were exciting for me because good morning started a new day. A new day to do it all over again.

May 8, 2020

I know we're supposed to look forward, but I have been reflecting a lot lately—some parts of my past that I totally regret, but some that I'm glad it's over. I'm glad that I'm doing good, but I got so dizzy today, which reminded me that I still have POTS. I'm not okay, but I'm okay with not being okay today.

May 9, 2020

Today is here. It's been a complete year since my surgery. I'm happy that it was a successful year considering that I am not drunk or batshit crazy! This lame-ass dude had the audacity to ask me why I haven't called him. I don't care anymore; I have my own things to put in order. I was not a priority and you are not mine. I told him that shit hit different when it's your turn to go through it. I cleaned the entire house thinking about when is a great time to tell him that I no longer wanted to be bothered by him or anything he had been going. Besides, he is still a selfish asshole. It's all about him. He's finally with his child, where he needs to be. I believe that it's my turn to step back and let God take over. I felt so much anxiety because I wanted to celebrate with my mom, but she is getting what she needed, and I feel contented with that. I feel completely different this time of year. Of course, physically, but my mentally is up to par too. My self-esteem has reached a bad-ass 50 percent since this bullshit last year. I had a bunch of just-in-case dudes lined up if the people whom I wanted didn't want me. I would entertain the thought until the hurt subsided about being rejected. There has always been my little friend who consistently called and texted me just to see how I was doing. I appreciated it because since I was literally in the hospital, he never stopped checking on me.

May 10, 2020

It's the anniversary of my aunt's death. I'm still lost for words. Shit still hurts the same, nothing different except that it has been a full year. I literally cleaned everything I can possibly think of in this house. I guess it's time to focus on myself and truly clean up some baggage that doesn't belong to me. Okay, some might be mine too, some shit I created for myself, like continuing to feed these unhealthy relationships, including family. Never realized that it's okay not to like everyone and no doesn't mean never, just not right now. I can live with it or without it. God's blessing is not always an answered prayer in the way we want—truest statement ever made. Tell God your plans and see what happens. I spoke to my mom today. Greatest gift on Mother's Day. I miss her presence. What is time when you don't use it? I keep waiting for something to happen in my life. Please don't misunderstand me, I keep waiting for something to happen like in the movies. When you're writing and something magical appears and you figure out the mystery of your life. I've been experiencing some life-changing things, though. People whom I thought were friends turned out to be one-night stands that stood around too damn long. I take some ownership in it because I could have said that enough is enough and parted ways, but I let it drag on too. I guess I wanted something more from it too. I want to be clear that I wasn't always a good friend either. I had my shit too. Apologies were very few to none. I had to understand too that just because you apologize does not mean that you will be good friends again or things will be the same. People have different experiences. I may only remember hurting you once, but for someone else, it could have been several things to create distance, as I, too, remember the distances I put between people. I love the feeling of not surviving but now living. It is a sense of peace that only few can understand.

May 13, 2020

Another sleepless night. I'm always up thinking, wondering if I'll ever be able to reach those long-distance dreams and fantasies that consume my time. I often think about being able to provide for my son and family in a manner where things would be easier for us all. Money doesn't always change the scenario, but it damn sure makes things better and it comes with advantages. This pandemic and the number of deaths are sickening. We're faced with a president who does not care about people. If you were unclear about the "people," I mean poor American people. I worry about the children who went to school for peace against hunger and violence. I've never physically harmed my child, but I once was that parent who was drunk when he got home most days or blacked out that I could not feed him because I could not get up. I hate those things about me, but alcohol was my weakness. I didn't even like alcohol, but it was the quickest way to numb the pain that consumed me every day. I didn't even know that I had an alcohol problem because I went to work, washed my clothes, cleaned up, and helped my son with his homework. I just thought that I had drunk too much when I did drink. I convinced myself that I didn't have a problem because I did not drink every day. In those days that I did, I'm sure I had alcohol poisoning; there was no limit to what and how much I drink if I could only ignore this silent yet loud behavioral pain. I was okay, or at least that's what I thought. I've met a lot of people on my new journey and most of them have no idea about the experiences I had before. I say experiences because majority of the people say the person they used to be, but technically you are still the same person. It is no longer your experiences that hold you. Yes, you still have those scares and memories, but you do not have to remain a hostage of what you once endured. Honestly, most of the scares I have are things and situations that I created, and I hated others for not protecting me against my own demons. I was sick to my stomach because I wanted to stop drinking, but people would offer me just one drink, and I obliged because I thought that I could handle the impossible. I've been *ashamed* of those experiences because I adore who I am now. I have so much respect, honesty, ambition, morals, and trust for myself now that anyone who gets in between those must go. I also acknowledge the past and the bullshit I've done. This pandemic has really been good for me because it has given me time to be open about who and what I want out this situation. I do believe that God has sat us all down to become closer to him. I will say that I've strayed a few times. I owe God my everything, and my son deserves the world. I have someone in my life that truly loves me, and I love him too. It's not too fast or slow. He understands me in so many ways. I need to show up a little more because if he did stop calling, I would be crushed. He unquestionably shows me that he cares for me, my son, and my mom. I find myself starving for him, just something like to look and admire him. His affection sometimes scares me. I don't want to let my guard down and be disappointed yet again. Even though this is first time that I don't question everything. *Fuck*! I'm blissful and loving it. This is a joy that I won't share with everyone. It's nothing to hide, but some people will never let you enjoy a good time. My closest friends know all about him. Thank God for friendships! Family and time do not qualify for my friendship, and this applies for me as well. I used to assume that family was supposed to let you know everything, and because you had time with people, it earned you their business. Nope! My new journey has indicated that you must put the work in with friendship and romance. I told my closest girlfriends that I am smitten by my friend. Who the hell says smitten?—someone who is in awe.

May 23, 2020

Today has been weird but good. My friend and I have been constantly talking. We're good. The discussion of marriage came up. For the first time in history, I was not afraid or felt like running or dying about this topic. Has my maturity hit a growth spurt? The last time this conversation happened, things ended. I was not ready nor interested in the relationship anymore. Things were moving too fast, not mention I had no voice in the relationship. I used to be so vocal and opinionated that I chose to be laid-back and let him lead. Worst mistake of my life, not that I let him lead on accident, because I knew that I didn't have a leader. I was used to picking up the pieces. His bullshit was familiar, and at that time I lived successfully in chaos. Anything normal was an abscess that needs to be exposed. I focused a lot on what men needed to change so that I would be *happy*, not realizing that I carried the manual with me every day. All I had to do was look in mirror and pray for guidance. Anyway, the topic was different because it may happen this time around. He's worth the long days thinking about and dealing with the little things that don't make sense, but you still love him. Yup, that is where I am.

May 24, 2020

OMG! My son is fifteen years old today. I literally have fifteen years of experience of being a parent. I love every minute of it. The mistakes and milestones, all of it. The best part about being a parent is when you make a mistake and your child still loves you despite of it. My son has really come a long way from where he was. I love him unconditionally, and he will never know what it feels like to go without it. *Love* is an obligation and a privilege most people will never experience. Happy birthday, Kyree, Mommy's baby forever.

May 28, 2020

Wow! Time passed by fast when you're not paying attention or be mindful of it. So much has changed. My mom took a different turn with her health. I was surprised to see things suddenly change, but life teaches all of us a valuable lesson. Things can happen to anyone; no one is exempted from suffering or enduring unfair changes in life. We know that life has a way in doing things, and we know that every day will not be filled with sunshine, but we're never ready for a storm. That's why you praise him in advance. It's like a savings account where you put money in for a rainy day or when something unexpected happens. You rely on that, right? Praise God in advance, the outcome is still the same. It's easy to thank God when life is good, or if you're in a bind, you call his name. We tend to forget about praising him for those things we often forget about, like those secrets that no one knows or those embarrassing moments that only you and God witnessed. You know what I'm talking about. Thank him!

June 13, 2020

Wow, I finally said it. I admitted that I want to date someone else. Not that I haven't dated other people, but we tend to end up back at the same page when elsewhere doesn't work. I was open about my feelings with my oldest special friend. I was open, but I wasn't honest. We played this game over seven years now and my feelings are still the same for him. Except when things don't go my way, I run, and I hate it when I returned, I see that the pot of gold has grown. More chips were added, but after counting, it wasn't enough. I wanted to move on to see if the grass was greener on the other side. Benjamin Franklin looks the same on a hundred-dollar bill no matter how many times they reprinted it. I kept going back expecting a new result. Why couldn't he be the man I wanted and needed? *Potential is not acceptable.* When it comes to the matters of the heart, I was comfortable with potential because that was what I was giving out— potential. Looking back, I probably loved twice. Sometimes I feel bad because I was not always this woman with a lot of dudes; I crossed paths. Most of them will never know the improved Mercy. Fuck it! They didn't deserve this greatness. Okay, maybe I'll apologize a little for the old version of me; she was unapologetically damaged. I still have those wounds, but the salt falls off easily now. Today, I was sleepy, but I was thankful to have a job, especially with the pandemic and people losing their jobs every day. I can't wait to hear

Kyree's plan to do some creative thinking. I love seeing him being passionate about something. Oh! I must thank Alice for introducing me to Jane; she had open-heart surgery too. I can tell that her heart was as welcoming as her smile. God bless her.

June 16, 2020

Today has been an eventful day of bullshit. My boss called me asking if I will be in tomorrow. I told her that I had things do. Since we returned to the building, our schedules had been crazy. They put you where they want, places where they do not feel like doing it themselves. I am totally paranoid of opening back to the public. I go out every day, but it is at my own risk and caution. That is where my point lies—I do not like working for someone else. I feel like an idiot working hard every day for a minimum wage. Granted that I have salary, I sat at home a few months and made more than I do working hard. In this place, you must dedicate yourself to the cause. It's a great ideal thing, but you must be willing to give up anything and anyone to be successful here. Unless you are higher-ranked, you're not getting paid your worth. I heard people saying how disappointed they were because they were not given raises or bonuses; I cannot blame them. People work hard and never get compensated for their worth.

June 17, 2020

Today is the day that I spend quality time with my special guy. I really like this dude. I could name forever why. We never have enough time together, but the space does make the heart grow fonder. I'm back working, so late nights and early mornings are over. This time showed me that the small things matter too.

June 18, 2020

Coming to work early was easy. Things were calm and at ease. We attended a training that I thought was good, considering we open Wednesday night and despite asking questions and never getting the answers you needed. But it was best said that the people who don't do the work always say that it's easy. Today is June 18 and some states made it a paid holiday. That's nice, but when will we (Black folks) ever be paid for unwanted slavery? They continuously give us holidays, but nothing more. While at work, I often daydream about my life being different. I can also taste the new life. I just have to keep going, pushing forward. I see the happiness and myself enjoying the fruit of my labor. I remind myself to take at least an hour to dedicate to my future. I can see the light, but I must create a path there. No one will ever care about your dreams as much as you.

June 21, 2020

Woke up praying that I was a billionaire. I had an amazing dream. I was finally earning the money I deserved, married, had a daughter, and Kyree was off to a great start in life. Oh no! I'm not. Oh well, time to shower and get my day started. I noticed how I was draining my own energy. I hated everything about work, except a few people. Some people will always remain on my list of good people. This one lady, Melissa, reminds me of the old alcoholic that I used to be—very sneaky and conniving. I say "used to be" because I'm a recovering alcoholic. I wasn't fooled; I've seen it all before. She could have the potential to be great, but she is so in her own way that she can't see it. She has those qualities no one respects. She claims that she's by the book. She's not upfront; she'll laugh in your face while she's marking where she'll throw the knife in your back. The management here sucks; they don't care about their employees, except maybe one person. It's COVID-19, where are the accommodations to make your staff feel safe. A cheap tent and a fan, really? What a fucking joke! This new guy, Marvin, keeps coughing. I wonder where it comes from or maybe those cigarettes, as he tries to sneak in a smoke when he thinks no one is watching, then comes back reeking of cologne and cigarette smoke. He's a very arrogant man. Sometimes I feel like what I do here isn't enough. I do things and they are still overshadowed by bullshit. It is always a new rule here; nothing is the same. I adapt well to changes and situations. I knew that COVID-19 would be different, but who knew that the changes would affect your well-being? One minute they are screaming that we need more people, and then the next, we need to cut on employees and expenses. I've been actively looking for new jobs, but things are slow in seeking new employment. There is no security here. I often think about my relationship and where this may go. I don't want to be staggering forever. I'm not pushing for things to move fast, but I am open to settling down and having a kid, preferably a girl, but I would love just the same if God blessed me with another boy. The thought of three guys, sheesh!

June 23, 2020

Today was very weird for me. I am sitting next door to the CEO of my job. She is an easy person to talk to. Most would not agree, but I like her. Many people spend their time kissing her ass; they cannot get to know her or what she stands on. It's refreshing to see the top dogs in here. I was shocked myself because I didn't think that they did things like this. It may have been for show. To be continued.

Remember I told you how proud I was about seeing the top dogs showing up and doing their so-called dues? It was bullshit! She took picture of herself as if she was really working. It was simply showing face. There was no real bloodwork. I wasn't too upset because I got to leave due to casual conversation and always carrying my customer service skills with me on and off the clock. I am not sure if I am lucky or picky about the position I am in, but I hated not having money, so

I work. It always tortures me because my freedom is taken. I know they say that we make a difference in people's lives as a good and position thing, but why work to the bone, yet still not satisfied? I guess work will always be work if you don't love it. I don't love it. It literally drives me crazy working for someone else and living by their rules, even if it is temporary. But remember when you have dreams and you're working toward them, things are only temporary.

June 25, 2020

I really had to check myself. I am so used to things always being about me that I sometimes forget that I am in a relationship/friendship. Granted yesterday my friend did not tell me that he went to a funeral, somehow I woke up feeling like he owed me more. I was so selfish, but somehow the story seemed fishy because it was his sister's ex-boyfriend or fling. He never mentioned that someone died. Hell, I've never seen his friends. I did not think or realize that men go through things too. It is embedded that men should always be strong, but they are built with the same emotions. Of course, men display emotions different. I regrouped myself and remembered how I felt when things were not always positive and how I wanted someone in my corner. I reached out and we are in a good place. Something tells me that he got over me. I'll let it slide for now. Note to self (catch his ass later). I can feel the distance in between us already.

June 27, 2020

I was happy to wake up again. Thank you, Jesus, for your ever mercy. At the same time, I hated the feeling of not speaking to my special friend. Oh! So wait, I never told you what happened yesterday. I was sitting at work when I realized that my special friend never reaches out to me unless I contact him first. Granted before I went back to work, he would do an excellent job at communicating. When I went back to work, he called me once, but I could not answer. I was in the room full of VPs and a CEO. He did not like that at all. After that, he never called again, unless I was home late and he wanted to vent about something that happened or just about him in general. Back to the story. I was sitting at work when I realized that my special friend does not reach out to me anymore. It was always me who does the texting and checking in. So I decided to jokingly let him know so I would not come off harsh. Boy did I get shut down! I clearly stated what I needed from him, and he gave me every excuse why he has not. I was not looking for him to defend why he was not, but to hear my plea of me missing and wanting him to acknowledge it. He gave me a complete itinerary of what he did, which I did not ask for; it was a way to justify him not reaching out and to make me look bad.

He told me:

He got his hair cut.

He was taking care of some business.

He was at a candlelight vigil for his friend (which happens to be his sister's old boyfriend or fling); questionable, but whatever! This was supposed to be your sister's ex-boyfriend whom she loved for years and y'all were like brothers. She didn't go to the funeral or candlelight vigil, yet you never even mentioned this guy.

After all these things of knowing, he suddenly switched the topic to shoes. Since he seemed to be over everything, I thought that it would be a good time to mention my text. He immediately lets me know how he is and not worry about what I'm talking about because he has a lot of shit on his mind. I believe that he does have a lot going on. But not once in a whole week that he ever thought to tell me or ask how I was doing, how my day was, or if I am okay. I totally get it now—it is a selfish relationship until you need me, then it moves to a we (thing). Nope! I am always validated in any place or situation.

No one dictates how I am valued. If you are not making me anything but great, I do not want you around me, period. I want to be very distinct. I can take constructive criticism, but you must mean well when doing so, not just to get me quiet. I told myself that I would work on managing how I say things, but I would not be doing myself any justice holding back how I truly feel. I replayed some situations over in my head just to make sure that I was not overreacting, but my feelings are still manifesting, which to my expertise means that it's certified. I am not saying that he does not know how to love. I am just saying that he does not know how to love me the way I need and want yet. I used "yet" because I want to be sure that I thoroughly explained my needs and wants. If he does not fulfill what I need, then we will go our separate ways. I do not believe in beating a dead horse. Hell! You can lead a horse to the well, but you cannot make him drink. With all that has been said, my feelings were sincerely hurt. On my standpoint, I was not being heard and that is what hurts the most. It is dreadful knowing that my best time to write is when someone withholds care for my feelings. Do I live well in chaos? Nah! I see growth in a peaceful environment. Maybe the rainbow will shine again.

July 21, 2020

Today was new, but I was determined to be pissed. I started thinking about all the things that my special friend told me, and things started to fall apart yet come together for me. This fool didn't really want me. He knew that I had connections to any drug he wanted. I put him up with people and places that he never went. He may have wanted something genuine in the beginning, but after he showed me his small stash, I was tickled pink at the thought of him, thinking he was doing something sizable. I continued to watch as he placed his grams on the scale and cursed out any crackhead who got bold enough to tell him what he would and wouldn't do. I was not okay with this, but I figured that we were in the middle of a pandemic and he lost his job, so this would be temporary. I remembered him telling me there's no good coke on the streets and everything's basically some bullshit. I knew in my heart that I should have remained quiet and let him talk himself off the bridge, but no, I had to come with my shit. I spoke up and said, "I know some people. What are you looking for? And by the way, you are cooking it wrong. Don't nobody cook it in the microwave." I introduced him to some folks and now I created a monster. But deep down inside I was proud. It was potential and fearlessness that I couldn't do for myself. Realest ever, those who can't, teach.

July 23, 2020

Woke up this morning feeling okay. Work is miserably boring at times. Entertainment depends on who is here. I dyed my sister's hair today and it turned out beautifully. I did a wonderful job. I just found out that her schedule changed. I knew that nothing would last forever, but damn! I started to feel a rush of anxiety. I knew that I could not rely on her anymore. Not like she didn't care, but my illness was comfortable knowing that she was around. I needed to focus on how to stand on my own. I'm not a punk, but I need to find my own way. I'm so nervous about this new travel life by myself. My strength is where I live; that's how I conquer every day, good or bad. I have my faith, but I just know that it will not be easy. I wish I had to the things and money to hire someone to drive me where I need to go. If and when I do come across some good money, I will add that in someone's yearly salary so I would be good for a year, without worrying about how I will get around or depending on someone else for my safety. I feel disgusted when I must ask people for help. I was thanking the Lord every day for slowly getting me around, but I'm dying miserably on the inside. I crumbled on how I felt and how I feel when I put up a fight every day that I'm okay. I contacted a free disability evaluation line just to see if I may qualify. Of course I didn't, because I'm still working. I feel like shit every day, but respecting and saying that it's okay to be weak is nonnegotiable. I need money to finance myself and my child. Every day I pray that I don't die. I held myself together like no other with God's mercy. In some moments, I count the seconds before I feel like I'm going to die. Lord, I am nervous that this (POTS) thing only gets worst in the physical form.

July 25, 2020

Today, I felt so insecure and foolish at the same time. I lied and told my friends that my boyfriend was going to a pool party, then changed his mind as if he thought about me. I was uncomfortable when he told me. I should have said something, but then I thought that I might be overreacting with my own insecurities. I was, but let's be clear, he made sure to let me know that just about every woman there had a beautiful body, but he didn't look at any of them in that manner. I was feeling insecure because I gained some weight, but now I can truly say that my weight has moved in other unsatisfying places. I wear a denim jacket around my waist to distract people from looking at my stomach. I can honestly feel the extra weight. It was cute at first, but I see me going down a road which I'm not ready. I thought I felt uncomfortable, but it was my own insecurities feeling like I wasn't good enough. Every man has complimented my weight gain, but now I see me moving in a different light. Obscenity is something, I fear. Weight gain was something I prayed for and now I'm afraid to gain another pound. I go places where guys are always flirting, so it wasn't the pool party. It was me feeling like I wasn't enough to keep his attention when I'm worthy of any man no matter who they are. I'm my own trophy and best prize, hands down. My special friend secures my flaws every day, but he also knew how to insult my security in the same breath. Thinking about it now, he never invites me anywhere, except to complement a drug deal, but always out and about. Okay, I wasn't butt-hurt about not being invited; ending deals were my best parts. I spent that shit as fast as I got it. I'm a shopaholic. Besides, I was running out of bullshit to tell my mom anyway. Through all the chaos, I still wanted to be treated like a lady. I knew that was I special and worthy to be treated as such. I just could not figure out how to apply pressure when it meant the most to me. Something is brewing in the air. I feel the shift coming soon.

July 26, 2020

Man, I kept myself together. I went back and forth in my head, whether he's being faithful or if he's having a good time and remembering that he has a woman who's down for him regardless. Not regardless with cheating, but through the other storms. Damn! I thought my shit was getting better and here I am fighting insecurities that don't belong to me. I'm willing to trust, so I'm delivering these Jane Doe packages to whom they belong. I no longer want it; it's too heavy. Lord, I pray that you keep me in good company with a clear heart. Besides, I'm dope as hell. Okay, I admit it, I'm not convinced that nothing happened at the pool party. He has a pattern and it's not following through. I'm a vibe person and the atmosphere has shifted. It's almost 1 p.m. and I haven't heard nothing from him. Maybe I can call him to check on him, especially since he didn't text once he got home. His ass okay? He just did what he wanted to do. I'm not his wife, so I keep my opinions to myself, but I thought you were to *speak up* if you have something that bothers you. I haven't called because I try not to bother. Damn! I thought I was okay with it. I guess I let other people's opinions get into my head. Nah, I didn't like it, but he's a grown man, he knows what he should do, and I trust with no regards, unless one shows me otherwise. He keeps bringing up this lady named Kissy. Kissy is supposed to be his cousin's girlfriend/ex-girlfriend. Why did you attend a pool with your cousin's girlfriend? Oh! His cousin wasn't there either. He talked about all the men who complimented Kissy on her curves and accessories. He told me that Kissy is nothing to worry about because she's an older woman and he doesn't look at her that way. She's an old friend whom he hooked up with his cousin, Curtis. Oh! Did I tell you that Kissy also bailed my special friend out of jail? Curtis never knew about this incident. Okay, I know they fucked before. He never admitted to me, but come on, a woman's intuition is never wrong no matter how hard we try to block the feeling. Well, you're a damn fool if you don't trust that feeling because I know plenty of older guys who look good and stunning. They might not be my speed now, but if things ever changed, I might smash. If I were invited, I would go with my friends too, except it wasn't his friends. It's my own insecurities, and some people enjoy seeing you in an ugly place. I never needed the details. He wanted me to feel like I was in a competition with this woman. He described her as being cool as one of my oldest aunts, yet she had a body like a popular video vixen, and you weren't interested. Stop dropping off your packages, I don't want it. Hell, I barely know what you're upset about, but you pass the buck so easily.

June 29, 2020

Woke up ready to address every issue I had the previous day. I dressed super cute and sounded wonderful to nature's ears. My special friend picked me up and every wrong disappeared, not because I was stupid or naïve to anyone or anything, but because he immediately addressed it by apologizing, as his usual routine of bullshit and truly stepping up to be an extreme gentleman. He better get used to doing these things, because I do return the favor as well. We had a wonderful day. We laughed and flirted like high school kids, but the feeling was magical. I truly love this guy. It's so easy and normal, but we are far from normal. I adore our process of things. Okay, I was in love with the situation, not him. We find our way every day and every day fulfilled. There's nothing sexier than a man who listens and applies what you said to your routine. That's not the case here. I hate his fucking guts. He's a liar, but I thought to myself, *why not get a free meal and a few pair of shoes to walk out his life in?* I've upset him and he has done the same, but nothing's worth walking around fighting and arguing. Life is too short. I'm wondering what or where we would be if I had given him a chance long before now. Oh! Who cares? Look at me now, picking up the pieces that I didn't even want for real. Most days, I am super nervous and scared because I am open, like open to love. I have said that I loved men; most that I had love for were like, I genuinely cared about them. But this kind of *love* is something I never experience. I'm sober. I dream in the day and desire in the night. Not just sexually, but everything about *love* moves me in a different direction for a greater me. I reconsider the people I hang around. It's an energy thing. Will I ever get this kind of *love* to anyone?

July 2, 2020

Some ways about him are mature and relatable. Other times, he knows exactly how to relate to my son, which can be a blessing and a curse. Of course! You want your child to be comfortable around someone you're dating, but there should be a line drawn when they dress alike.

July 3, 2020

I woke up not completely my best. I know I've been working a little more than usual. I need to make sure that I put myself first, especially when it comes to my health. COVID-19 has no special person in mind. I'm doing sixteen-hour shifts while I watch my bosses go home before sunset. I must get out of this situation—working under someone else's thumb is not my ideal dream of living the dream. Fuck this place. I should get up and walk out the door. Do it! Get up! Shut up, rent's due in two days.

July 7, 2020

I was completely done with everything; my health showed its natural ass today. I felt every symptom of POTS. Nothing was okay today. For the first time, I was okay with not being okay. I spent the day in bed.

July 28, 2020

I woke up feeling inspired to keep writing even in the midst of thinking poorly. I saw a text message from one of my staff members saying that she needed a day away. I was immediately pissed until I realized that she would help my nerves better at home than here. Our temp (branch) manager, what a fucking jerk! I'm not sure if he did something personal to me, but he rubs me the wrong way every time he speaks. He does not say inappropriate things. It's his demeanor that speaks for itself: I'm a fucking jerk and there's nothing you can do about it. I could get up and walk out, but I'll be doing myself damage with no income. I pray to God for protection over my loved ones. It's been working as I continue with that prayer I need to add in more dedication to my own goals. I want to be heard. I was in such denial when I found out that I had to have open-heart surgery. My body completely went numb and my mind checked out. I told myself that I would document my journey through the time I was in the hospital, and now I realize that I was recovering from my addiction. It came with many stimulations, though. Sex, hangovers, mood swings, and secrets I'm taking to my grave. I told you some things, but God knows you wouldn't be able to handle the unspoken truth about silent cries that linger with me every step.

July 29, 2020

Man, today was chilled considering most people were home. My special friend called me at 4 a.m. I was concerned because only bad news happen after 12 a.m. I called, but he didn't answer. I assumed something was wrong. As to why, you would understand that everything was always nerve-racking in my life at this moment. When I finally heard from him, he starts explaining some shit I didn't even ask for at all. Before he got finished, I had to let him know that he called me first and I was only checking on him. He's been very fussy and antsy lately. I think he's dipping in his own stash for play. I told him on Monday how I've been feeling about the way he's been treating me. I told him that I feel like I don't have a place in his life. Yes, you claim me as your woman to people who don't even know my real name, but the actions are all different. If someone calls, he must go. I'm never the choosing point. He acknowledged my feelings and apologized. At least I thought the shit didn't change much. This is starting to become a normal routine: I'll do what I want and apologize later; I'll gift her with a nice dinner and something fancy to shut her up; when I call, he never answers; when he calls, it is all about him, and I cannot remember the last time he genuinely asked me about me, like my day or if I ate. I ask every day, sometimes twice a day, because I know that he does not focus on eating right. He called today and of course it was all about him. He decided to go to the bar with his friends as a man who supposedly doesn't drink. He's been drinking heavy lately too. He said he'll call me back. When he said that, it reminded me of a friend who asked about a good bar with frozen drinks. I called back and asked the name, but before I got the chance to ask, this dude says, "Why are you calling me back when I said I'll call you? What's up?" What? I was so pissed that I hung up and didn't call or answer for a while. I am a hell of a woman. I try my hardest not to unload my unnecessary baggage on anyone. I refuse to be treated as if I were your second choice in anything. I will not answer my phone for two days. If I miss him that much, then maybe it's worth keeping around. If I survive and feel okay, then I'll take a break and things will change. I am not playing merry-go-round with my heart anymore. I know my worth and what I'm capable of doing and bringing to any relationship, not just personal. I'm very observant even when I'm talking, I peep shit. I move off vibes and patterns, and his ultimately shifted.

July 30, 2020

Man, I started talking to someone else. Not in a romantic way, but something to pass the time. Okay, that was bullshit! I wasn't really into the guy. I just needed to feel wanted and appreciated again. I knew that nothing would come out of this, but I felt satisfaction in knowing that I haven't lost my touch. It also reminded me that I have options too. I'm nobody's fool. I sent my special friend a long message after he apologized as he always does. I told him how special I was. The only thing was I wasn't sure if I was convincing him or myself. I was, without a doubt, trying to convince myself. I wanted what I wanted. I hated not getting it. If I feel that I wasn't getting what I desired, then you must pay. I know exactly how I want to be treated. He used to make me feel alive, not that I was dead without him, but love brings a new foundation of life to you. He texted me saying that I was right. I didn't want to be right. I wanted to be treated like I was in the beginning. There was no better feeling. It's crazy that he mistreats me, and here I was thinking and praying that he will be okay. I started missing him, so I texted to see if he was okay. He told me that he would call me in a minute. It was 3:06 p.m. and he never called. I called and got my answer. No answer is an answer. Let's just say that I'm hurt, but I'm crushed. Every time I think I did it the right way, I lose. I was winning inside because now the relationship is becoming boring. I have officially reached my fun point. I'm starting to feel something and this is where it gets tricky for me. I'm horrible at emotions, very detached, and loves being alone, unless I invite you into my world. Even then, I enjoy my freedom with no question asked. No, it's not a cheating thing, but I do enjoy playing by my own rules. It's probably my time to focus on myself and get my health under control. Now, I have another man that I must discontinue myself from as well. It hasn't been many, barely a few, but

I just got to be embarrassed again! I cut so many people off to focus on this dude. I honestly thought that he would be my biggest project yet. He was perfect. He dressed well, no kids, never been married, and he wasn't as smart as he thought he was about street life. He was socially retarded and I knew it. Anyway, I always bounce back. But maybe this is my time to sit down and manifest my life and where I want to go. I thought we had plans together, but apparently I'm not enough or only on his time. I'm good enough for me. This shit hurts, but I am going to keep pushing because I know there's a rainbow at the end. I have the biggest tears and lump in my throat, but I refuse to give away another tear on anyone who doesn't think I'm enough. Okay! Yes, that was a whole production that I just wrote. Things are not that bad. I tend to forget that people have their own shit that they go through too. A little over a year and I'm okay with not drinking to clear my head. Not that I haven't been thinking about it, but I'm okay with living through the burn of the hurt. A part of me knows that I deserve better; it's the 50 percent of me, that little abandoned girl, who hates to feel rejected. So I sometimes endure the pain of others just to avoid any hurt with a hint of honey. I see people working toward their plans or at least seem to know what they want to do with their lives. My biggest dream is to have a clothing line after selling my journey. Thanks for reading thus far!

July 31, 2020

Guess what? My special guy and I had a long talk. We understand how things can be, but we also know that we have love for each other and that matters most. He was talking about "I don't argue with you, I let you say what you need, and that's it." Even through all the mess, he apologizes and acknowledges my feelings after I cool off. I will say that he tries to bullshit a bullshitter, which is always a win in my book. Or am I believing what I want to so things seem better than they are? I didn't care, I just needed to get through the day. I knew that I created something more powerful than me this time around.

Most of the time, men would eventually switch over and notice the differences in themselves, but he enjoyed the savage that he became.

August 5, 2020

Today has been great. I woke up feeling refreshed like something new happened. My special guy and I are in a very good place. I fed the bear a great meal after a million speeches, as he calls it. LOL. I believe he gets it. I love him dearly. He really tries and his effects are noticeable. I truly appreciate him. He knows that I'll be around because we have a common like for the same things. He genuinely cares. Ha! I called his bluff. That fool was really trying to secure a place in my life to cause damage. I see you lurking around the corner doing the bare minimum to keep a seat at my table. Come on, self-esteem, we're better than this. Why are we here? Am I still this abandoned little girl searching for Daddy in every man who stands six feet one or better? Or do you dare to challenge yourself and every man to be a better version of himself the next time around? Anyway, some days my health is great, like today I only had a few dizzy spells. Yesterday was horrible; my anxiety wouldn't fold. Every time I found myself being calm, it flared right back up. I felt totally sick most of the day, then at nighttime, it became much better. That's the things with POTS—one day it's great, the next it's awful for days. Most days, I battle with pretending to look okay and not looking sick. It's clear that I can fight a battle with the blood of Jesus on me. Amen. I thank God for good seconds that he provides for me. Good or bad beats being dead. I daydream often now because I ponder my future. I want a comfortable life. A nice house and two or three kids. I really want a girl to bond with. I love my son unconditionally; that's my firstborn baby. He'll always be my baby. I now understand the difference in raising girls and boys. A woman could never show a boy how to prepare or become a man. All you can do is keep the right people around them. Not to mention teenage boys are gross. They only think about girls, phones, friends, and sometimes sex. I know that's a scary word for some parents, but it's true. That's some boys. I pray to God for protection and guidance in a world so cruel to Black men. I don't know what it's like to raise a girl, but my mother did an excellent job with the tools that she had. Of course, I wanted more! Three meals and a cox were luxury items where I'm from, but I always had a vision. I want to be the person reaching until I'm the person that becomes hard to contact. I just couldn't get past the liquor; it was my pacifier and safe place for secrets along with a broken spirit. I yearned for the bond of a healthy mother-and-daughter relationship. It wasn't toxic, but even when I ran to catch up, I couldn't close the gap. My son will forever be spoiled by his grandmother and me. I know it's difficult to let go, but boys hold on to something for their mothers, which I love. My mother became my realest best friend. She's down for whatever and would get me straight at the same time.

August 8, 2020

Today was awkward. I woke up ready for work. I was super tired and not feeling my best, but I pushed through. I finally told my girlfriend about me/her getting to work late, granted that I'm grown and I'm accountable for myself. I'm not sure what's been up with her lately, but I guess when the time is right, she'll come around and tell me. I've always had a reputation of being on time. I'm no longer comfortable with not controlling others, but I can control myself and how I do things. I can taste the difference in how my life is about to change. I think about my favorite performer and her work ethics. I see why she charged the amount for her concerts. She works hard and deserves it. So do I. Some days I don't want to do anything. That's truly okay. It's okay to do nothing. But hard work goes a long way. All of that is great. I'm not being truthful and I wish I would be as open to people as I can to you. But I thought my friend would have said more than you do. Do what you must do. I thought because we both had the same thing to do, she would notice things and want to change, but that comes with control. I cannot control others. It drives me crazy that most people don't have a sense of urgency. Well, let me change that. It's a sense of urgency for the things that I think are important. My livelihood is important. Even when I don't care, I show up. Anyway, moving forward. My feelings were kind of hurt because I've been constantly getting harsh words from her. I didn't expect someone so close to me say, "You should get someone or yourself to read it out loud, because people don't read anymore." Well, at least I don't. That was an opinion. That's like saying people don't take art serious no more that they will buy anything. I know what you're thinking—shots fired—but no, I was simply showing how I felt on the receiving end. I love her dearly and still wouldn't trade her for the world. I just see things in a different light. I can't wait to stand completely on my own two feet. I appreciate the love and effects of others, but depending on people slows you down. I hate feeling helpless, but I understand that no one can do it alone.

August 11, 2020

Today, I prayed for a different result. I didn't come to work expecting that today to be boring and useless like most days. I prayed that something good would happen today. I woke up and so did my family. I give my special friend a hard time sometimes, but it's all in me finding myself. I'm completely in love with myself. I haven't had this feeling in years. Even this feeling is different because I'm sober through it. I'm praying for something new. I pray for his protection, understanding, and patience. I love him for who he is, but patience is not his thing. I've seen a side of him that I think he was not ready to expose. He lost his temper, which we all do at times, but this time was beyond scary. I counted the seconds to my death as he approached this man's vehicle. I've never seen him get angry and upset, of course. The zero to one hundred was an understatement. I questioned my safety with him, as if selling drugs wasn't on the menu. I love the fast money, but I knew where I was headed. The thought of getting what you wanted and when you wanted did something to me. It was the rush of knowing that I could get it and not getting caught made the rules irrelevant. He wants a closer relationship with my son. I wonder, *Do I block it unknowingly?* My son thinks he's cool, but I'm very protective of who I allow in our life as a unit. Maybe I'm a little jealous that my son and him will bond greatly, then I would be left out. Not in a childish way, but there would be no one for me to talk to or hang around. A wonderful friend of mine called today. We Facetimed and it was exactly what I needed. His encouragement and dedication to our friendship means the world to me. He calls me on my bullshit and praise me when I'm doing good. He knows a lot of my demons and never once judged me for anything. There's nothing I wouldn't do for him. He's permanently in my life. You know how you sometimes do something and people tell you to use a placeholder to fill things up? He's not one of those things. I'm sure that we all have placeholders in our lives, something to fill up the holes, but it's always been different with this friendship. He never turned his back on me. Even when I was at my worst, he showed me that ugly can turn into a priceless piece. He's been there every step of the way. He was my lesson and blessing. I wonder if I . . .

August 18, 2020

I woke up and my head was hurting so bad. I got some cornrows and boy did I forget what it felt like when someone braids your hair. It looks beautiful but painful. Me and my special guy exchanged some words today. My mom was doing her business. I told my friend about my mom applying for disability. He interfered with the situation and I agreed with him, saying that we both could get the benefits due to our experiences. But of course, his surgery was serious compared to mine. I lay on a table dead for seven hours. Please don't downplay my experience. I never once or even considered thinking that it's just some simple surgery. We both endured trauma and had different experiences. I sent a long text message explaining how I felt, still acknowledging that we both went through something. No text or call. It's been a complete day. Yes, I called twice and now I feel completely stupid. For the first time ever in any relationship, I wasn't mad. I was hurting. Not drinking, I know what it felt like to be hurt. Honestly, it's not too bad that I keep getting by the minute. Usually, I would try anything to get someone's attention, but I'm too beautiful, smart, and talented to struggle through any relationship. When he needed me, I was right by his side. I told him that I needed to talk to him and he's nowhere to be found. It's a one-sided relationship when it comes to emotions and feelings. His are the ones that count. When he has a problem, I let him talk and say whatever he needs to say. When it's my turn, I'm crying or fussing as if what I said isn't valid. I have abandonment issues, but I'm never too hurt to let people treat me like shit! The old me would have needed answers, but no answer is an answer. Today, I was not okay. I was not okay with anything. Work was a blur and so were the conversation in between. My special guy friend finally called and it was all bullshit. He gave me a half-ass apology and I wasn't going for it. Why do I stay when I know that I don't like it here? Duh! It's familiar to me. I see myself in him. I like seeing how far he would go.

August 19, 2020

I called three times because I missed him through it all. He then gave me another weak-ass apology. He still didn't listen to how I truly felt about the situation. I just chose not to argue anymore. He made me wait on him. He called when he was ready to talk to me, not when we should or cared about how it made me feel. I now hold some resentment toward him and myself. I allowed him to disturb my peace. I was peacefully minding my business when he decided to enter my world. I let him in when it was the worst time of my life. I figured that he would understand due to the situation he had. But it's clear that this wasn't about surgeries or seat belts; this was about him wanting to spend his birthday elsewhere. Being a complete jackass was the first thing on the list. His stubbornness and temper can alert me, especially since we talked about children. He called me again, but at this point I'm past hurt, laughing, and mad. I'm back focusing on me. I don't want to ruin his birthday, so I kept my thoughts to myself. Well, I'm really sharing it with you. He wanted to share his birthday with other people. I've been asking for two months straight. When he finally did answer, it didn't include me. He made the decision for me, which meant he didn't want me around. Just because I don't drink doesn't mean that I don't know how to have a good time. He even mentions on the phone that if I wanted to argue, I could wait until after his birthday week. Oh! I forgot we had plans for the weekend. He wants to ruin it so I can be mad, and he does what he wants. He's a grown-ass man acting like a teenager. The next call, he says that he was in the gym his phone went dead. This fool has never seen the inside of a gym besides looking at mine at work. But anyway, I heard a loud noise in the background. I asked, "Was there someone blowing leaves?" Here he goes with the bullshit. Someone was vacuuming their car. He said, "Why are you so nosy?" as if I was checking on him. I can't hear. That was my final straw with him. I thought this man genuinely cared about me. It was all for show. If he wants to be in my life, he needs to do a lot of changes. Or do I need to make the changes myself?

August 25, 2020

Sheesh, it's been a rough week. I mean rough. I and my special friend have been in a bad place. Well, it's not a bad place, it's the "truth place." The truth place is where the true shows itself and we aren't ready to accept it, so we throw blame to avoid seeing the true color of a person or situation. When I wanted to talk about issues, he thinks it's an argument, which is nonsense. It's his way of ignoring the issue at hand. I just want to address things, so I don't harvest these feelings for later. I truly believe that this is my first real relationship, because I actually have feelings and I want to work thing out, but it's toxic and it can also be my karma. After all the shit I've done, maybe it's my turn to get back what I put out. I feel like he loves me equally. I also believe that he can be emotionally immature sometimes. I've been talking my friends' heads off about this. Thank God for friends. I told myself that I would keep my business to myself, but when you're hurting, your friends know, especially your real friends. I've really been doing the work to keep things going. I just don't see how you can be okay with not talking to the person you say "I love you" to every day at all. I hate arguing with myself, but I don't want to feel lost or complacent in my relationship. I see that when we do talk, he shuts down completely. He doesn't shut down from the conversation; he shuts down from the entire relationship. Do I think that he's cheating on me? Physically no, not at this moment. I believe that his interest has changed or moved elsewhere. Do I wish that he would talk to me more about things that bother him? Absolutely. Not just our relationship, but other things too, like I don't want to know the last minute that you've been frustrated because you have a lot on your mind. I want to be aware of these things so I can help or give you the space you need. Again, I reached out this morning with a text; I got one back. I decided to call because I wanted to make sure that I was putting forward the effort through all the hurt. He told me that he wasn't ignoring me; he was handling some important things. I said, "Okay, call me when you're done." He said okay, but this is the second day that he said that he would call and there's no further communication. Why am I holding on to everything that's broken? I know that he has a lot on his mind, but how do you not communicate with someone you love. There was a time when he would say "I love you" at least ten times a day and that he's in love with me. He wanted me to be so angry with him that if his friends made plans, he could do things for his birthday and give me the excuse that we were upset with each other. I would never lower myself to a place that makes you comfortable to be okay with dismissing or ignoring me. I became more intrigued about him because I saw myself acting out in his this-is-me-with-other-people behavior. I wanted to see more. Now, I hear that loud ringing that we're not capable of hearing as human beings. When things are completely quiet, you can hear all kinds of things. My gut feeling is fifty-fifty. One part is saying that you may not get what you want or deserve, so just walk away. The other part says, "Just give him time, he needs space too." I'm just missing the boat, though. I know that he has his phone, so how do you not say anything to the woman you love? Is he that busy, occupied, or going through something so deep that there's nothing to say? Or am I that blind and desperate that I'll make excuses for his ugly truth? He clearly doesn't want to be bothered much, and I don't know how to adjust. I talked to this man every day all day to no communication at all. Have I now met my match? I'm involved with myself through another person. POTS is still kicking my ass. There's no healing a beast.

December 31, 2020

It's been about four months or so today. I woke up in a blah mood. I finally realized that I pick low-impact men because I know what they're capable of. Not all are inadequate, but I know that their capacity to love can only reach a certain level, which requires me to do little as possible. When it comes to family and friends, I isolate myself to avoid any attachment when I feel comfortable. My entire adulthood, I have loved how my daddy showed me. Be inspired in the beginning and never be complacent. I'm what you call a modern-day sociopath. I purposely close off relationships so I cannot feel anything. *Do you forgive me?*

9 781664 178243